STUDY GUIDE
Volume I

THE AMERICAN JOURNEY

A History of the United States

TEACHING AND LEARNING CLASSROOM EDITION

FIFTH EDITION

David Goldfield
University of North Carolina, Charlotte

Carl Abbott
Portland State University

Virginia DeJohn Anderson
University of Colorado, Boulder

Jo Ann E. Argersinger
Southern Illinois University

Peter H. Argersinger
Southern Illinois University

William L. Barney
University of North Carolina, Chapel Hill

Robert M. Weir
University of South Carolina

Upper Saddle River, New Jersey 07458

© 2009 by PEARSON EDUCATION, INC.
Upper Saddle River, New Jersey 07458

10 9 8 7 6 5 4 3 2 1

ISBN 10: 0-13-603289-3
ISBN 13: 978-0-13-603289-2

CONTENTS

1
Worlds Apart

KEY TOPICS

✓ **America, West Africa, and Europe before 1492**
✓ **The Confluence of Three Cultural Traditions**

CHAPTER OUTLINE

I. Native American Societies before 1492
    A. Paleo-Indians and the Archaic Period
    B. The Development of Agriculture
    C. Nonfarming Societies
    D. Mesoamerican Civilizations
        1. The Mayans
        2. The Aztecs
    E. North America's Diverse Cultures
        1. Ancestral Puebloans
        2. Plains Indians
        3. Mound-building cultures
    F. The Caribbean Islanders

II. West African Societies
    A. Geographical and Political Differences
        1. Artisans and merchants
        2. Farming and gender roles
    B. Family Structure and Religion
    C. European Merchants in West Africa and the Slave Trade

III. Western Europe on the Eve of Exploration
    A. The Consolidation of Political and Military Authority
    B. Religious Conflict and the Protestant Reformation

IV. Contact
    A. The Lure of Discovery
        1. Advances in navigation and shipbuilding
        2. The Atlantic islands and the slave trade
    B. Christopher Columbus and the Westward Route to Asia
    C. The Spanish Conquest and Colonization
        1. The end of the Aztec Empire
        2. The fall of the Inca Empire
        3. Spanish incursions to the north
        4. The seeds of economic decline
    D. The Columbian Exchange
    E. Cultural Perceptions and Misperceptions

V. Competition for a Continent
    A. Early French Efforts in North America
    B. English Attempts in the New World
        1. The colonization of Ireland
        2. Expeditions to the New World
        3. The Roanoke colony

VI. Conclusion

SELF TESTING

Multiple Choice: In the blanks below, write the letter of the BEST response.

1. _____ When the Aztecs first sighted the fleet of Hernán Cortés, they regarded it as
    a. the second coming of a white messiah.
    b. an opportunity for trade with foreign merchants.
    c. an omen warning of trouble ahead.
    d. an impending invasion by Europeans.

2. _____ During the Archaic period, an "agricultural revolution" permitted
    a. a transition from a nomadic to a more settled society.
    b. a diversification of occupations.
    c. the development of religious beliefs.
    d. All of these occurred.

3. _____ Mesoamerica's most advanced writing, and calendrical systems were contributed by the
    a. Olmecs.
    b. Toltecs.
    c. Mayans.
    d. Aztecs.

4. _____ Among those cultures known as "mound builders" were the
    a. Hohokams.
    b. Anasazis.
    c. Adena-Hopewell.
    d. Mandans.

5. _____ Islam began to influence West Africa
    a. by the tenth century.
    b. especially among rural dwellers.
    c. especially among the merchant classes.
    d. as it lost influence in North Africa.

6. _____ Most Africans became slaves of other Africans because
    a. they had been captured in battle.
    b. they had been kidnapped.
    c. they were being punished for crimes committed.
    d. All of these reasons.

7. _____ Between 1300 and 1500, Europe was ravaged by all of the following EXCEPT
   a. the Hundred Years' War.
   b. the Black Death.
   c. malnutrition.
   d. invaders from North Africa.

8. _____ By 1492, most Europeans were
   a. landless peasants.
   b. small, independent farmers.
   c. merchants.
   d. lords and ladies.

9. _____ In 1492
   a. Spain completed the *reconquista*.
   b. the Portuguese began their Africa slave trade.
   c. Martin Luther initiated the Protestant Reformation.
   d. All of these are correct.

10. _____ One of the main reasons for Europeans' voyages of discovery was to
    a. bypass the Muslim-controlled Mediterranean.
    b. trade with the Native Peoples of the Americas.
    c. halt the spread of Protestantism.
    d. make slaves of Native Americans.

11. _____ Columbus thought he had traveled to Asia because of
    a. a malfunctioning steering mechanism.
    b. a woefully inaccurate map.
    c. a mathematical miscalculation of the size of the earth.
    d. All of these.

12. _____ French efforts to develop New World wealth were delayed because
    a. French rulers were preoccupied with European affairs.
    b. the earliest French attempts were disappointing.
    c. France was plunged into a religious civil war.
    d. All of these were reasons for the delay.

13. _____ The English monarch who created the Church of England was
    a. Henry VIII.
    b. Edward VI.
    c. Mary.
    d. Elizabeth I.
    e. James I.

14. _____ The first English child born in the New World was
    a. Francis Drake.
    b. Walter Raleigh.
    c. Virginia Dare.
    d. Richard Hakluyt.

15. _____ When Cabeza de Vaca returned to Mexico City, he was
    a. accompanied by a large army.
    b. hailed as a conquering hero.
    c. in possession of huge quantities of gold.
    d. lucky to be alive.

Chronological Arrangement: Re-arrange the list of events below by **re-writing** each item in correct chronological sequence into the blanks provided.

Founding of Roanoke   _____

Protestant Reformation begins   _____

Archaic Indian Era   _____

Viking Voyages   _____

Bering Strait Crossing   _____

Elizabeth I rules England   _____

Columbus "discovers" America   _____

Adena-Hopewell mound-builders   _____

Paleo-Indian Culture   _____

Coronado explores SW North America_____

Essay: Read each of the following questions, take some time to organize your thoughts, then compose thorough meaningful answers for each.

1. What political, cultural, economic, and social phenomena set the stage for Europe's exploration and exploitation of the New World?

2. What factors led European colonizers to adopt slavery as an important source of labor?

3. Describe the different elements that enabled the Spanish to conquer the Aztec Empire.

4. Discuss the "Columbian Exchange," listing and commenting upon each of the major "items" exchanged.

Map Identification: Use the map below to locate the following places:

Bering Strait   Pequots   Mandans
Anasazi/Pueblo   Iroquouis   Cheyennes
Adena/Hopewell   Cherokees   Apaches
Mayans   Crees   Modocs
Aztecs   Kiowas   Hopis

Map Identification: Use the map below to locate the following routes:

Cortés   de Vaca
de León   de Soto
Coronado   Balboa
Cartier

MULTIPLE CHOICE ANSWERS:

1. C	6. D	11. C
2. D	7. D	12. D
3. C	8. A	13. A
4. C	9. A	14. C
5. C	10. A	15. D

CHRONOLOGICAL ARRANGEMENT:

Bering Strait Crossing

Paleo-Indian Era

Archaic Indian Era

Adena-Hopewell mound-builders

Viking Voyages

Columbus "discovers" America

Protestant Reformation begins

Coronado explores southwestern North America

Elizabeth I rules England

Founding of Roanoke

2
Transplantation

KEY TOPICS

✓ **French and Dutch New World Colonies**
✓ **A Diverse Collection of English Colonies in North America and the Caribbean**

CHAPTER OUTLINE

I.   The French in North America
      A.   The Quest for Furs and Converts
      B.   The Development of New France

II.   The Dutch Overseas Empire
      A.   The Dutch East India Company
      B.   The West India Company and New Netherland

III. English Settlement in the Chesapeake
      A.   The Ordeal of Early Virginia
            1.   The Jamestown colony
            2.   The Powhatan Confederacy and the colonists
      B.   The Importance of Tobacco
      C.   Maryland: A Refuge for Catholics
      D.   Life in the Chesapeake Colonies

IV.   The Founding of New England
      A.   The Pilgrims and Plymouth Colony
      B.   Massachusetts Bay Colony and Its Offshoots
            1.   Stability, conformity, and intolerance
            2.   The Connecticut Valley and the Pequot War
            3.   Roger Williams and the founding of Rhode Island
            4.   Anne Hutchinson's challenge to the Bay Colony
      C.   Families, Farms, and Communities in Early New England
            1.   Women in early New England
            2.   Community and economic life

V.   Competition in the Caribbean
      A.   Sugar and Slaves
      B.   A Biracial Society

VI.   The Restoration Colonies
      A.   Early Carolina: Colonial Aristocracy and Slave Labor
      B.   Pennsylvania: The Dream of Toleration and Peace
      C.   New Netherland Becomes New York

VII. Conclusion

SELF-TESTING

Multiple Choice: In the blanks below, write the letter of the BEST response.

1. ____ According to his letter, the young English immigrant Richard Frethorne found all of the following in Virginia EXCEPT
   a. a prosperous new life.
   b. an unhealthy climate.
   c. starvation.
   d. fears of impending Indian attacks.

2. ____ Among the first French visitors to North America were those seeking
   a. fish.
   b. furs.
   c. Christian converts.
   d. All of these.

3. ____ Those Frenchmen who traveled and lived among Native People were known as
   a. *engages.*
   b. *filles du roi.*
   c. *seigneurs.*
   d. *coureurs de bois.*

4. ____ Most of the French who immigrated to Canada returned home.
   a. True.
   b. False.

5. ____ Which of the following was NOT a Dutch colony at one time?
   a. Ceylon (Sri Lanka)
   b. Sumatra
   c. New York
   d. Antigua
   e. the Spice Islands (Indonesia)

6. ____ Jamestown's "starving time" came largely as a result of the colonists'
   a. late arrival in 1607.
   b. arrival in a region too cold and barren to sustain them.
   c. preoccupation with finding gold.
   d. neglecting to provide for their own sustenance.
   e. Both c and d are correct.

7. ____ In 1619 the
   a. first women arrived in Virginia.
   b. first African slaves arrived in Virginia.
   c. Virginia House of Burgesses met for the first time.
   d. All of these occurred.

8. _____ The product that ultimately saved the Virginia colony financially was
   a. rice.
   b. cotton.
   c. tobacco.
   d. sugar.

9. _____ During the seventeenth century, the primary source of labor in Virginia was
   a. African slaves.
   b. white, English, indentured servants.
   c. large families with lots of children.
   d. Catholics fleeing persecution in neighboring Maryland.

10. _____ Most indentured servants ultimately became wealthy landowners themselves and then contracted with future would-be Virginians.
   a. True.
   b. False.

11. _____ Maryland originally was intended to be a refuge for English
   a. Quakers.
   b. Catholics.
   c. Puritans.
   d. Anglicans.
   e. Presbyterians.

12. _____ Family life was more stable in the Chesapeake area than in any other colonial region.
   a. True.
   b. False.

13. _____ John Winthrop told his Puritan followers that they were under contract to
   a. the Plymouth Company.
   b. King Charles I.
   c. God.
   d. the Church of England.
   e. the Massachusetts Bay Company.

14. _____ Roger Williams believed that Massachusetts churches were corrupt because they had not rejected
   a. the Plymouth Company.
   b. King Charles I.
   c. God.
   d. the Church of England.
   e. the Massachusetts General Court.

15. _____ The principal product of the Caribbean was
   a. rice.
   b. cotton.
   c. tobacco.
   d. sugar.

16. ____ The northern part of the Carolinas was suited to producing all of the following EXCEPT
   a. rice.
   b. lumber.
   c. tobacco.
   d. pitch.
   e. livestock.

17. ____ Quakers experienced persecution in England because
   a. of their informal worship services.
   b. they rejected the Calvinist notion of predestination.
   c. they granted women an unusual degree of equality in spiritual matters.
   d. they refused to acknowledge English social rank.
   e. All of these reasons are correct.

Chronological Arrangement: Re-arrange the list of events below by **re-writing** each item in correct chronological sequence into the blanks provided.

English Civil War   _____

Pennsylvania founded   _____

Plymouth Colony founded   _____

New Netherland becomes New York _____

Carolina founded   _____

First Africans arrive in Jamestown_____

Puritans found Massachusetts Bay_____

Charles II restored to English throne_____

Williams/Hutchinson banished   _____

James I becomes King of England_____

Essay: Read each of the following questions, take some time to organize your thoughts, then compose thorough, meaningful answers for each.

1. Why did mid-seventeenth-century New Amsterdam attract such a diverse ethnic and religious population?

2. Compare life in the seventeenth-century colonial Chesapeake region and in Colonial New England.

3. What problem(s) did the Puritans have with the Anglican Church (Church of England)?

4. Why were people such as Roger Williams and Anne Hutchinson not welcome in Massachusetts?

5. Discuss slavery in the colonial Caribbean. How did Africans preserve elements of a normal life?

6. Describe the circumstances in Europe that led to Jewish migration to the Americas, and their efforts to settle in the colonies.

Matching: Match each description in the left column with the person it most likely describes. (Beware: Not all names will be used!)

1. ____ First Stuart monarch in England; granted charters to the Virginia and Plymouth Companies.

2. ____ In 1681–1682, he descended the Mississippi River to its mouth; claimed its drainage area for France.

3. ____ Governor of New Amsterdam; seized the Swedish colony on the Delaware; surrendered to the English.

4. ____ Twenty-eight-year-old adventurer; imposed military discipline at Jamestown to avoid further starvation.

5. ____ Would-be friend—but later foe—of Jamestown; Father of Pocahontas.

6. ____ Married Pocahontas; introduced to Virginia a more palatable tobacco variety from Trinidad.

7. ____ Tried unsuccessfully to establish Maryland as a refuge for his fellow wealthy English Catholics.

8. ____ Puritan general whose protectorate governed England during its interregnum (1649–1660).

9. ____ English-speaking Native American; tried to function as mediator between the Pilgrims and Massasoit.

10. ____ Prosperous Puritan lawyer, governor of the Puritan colony; set forth their "errand into the wilderness."

11. ____ Separatist minister; banished from Massachusetts for opposing government interference in religion.

12. ____ Accused of "antinomianism;" held coed religious meetings in her home; moved to Rhode Island.

13. ____ Planned a tolerant society for his "woods," for fellow Quakers and for other oppressed Europeans.

A. Anne Hutchinson

B. Lord Baltimore

C. Charles I

D. Duke of York

E. Jonathan Edwards

F. Richard Frethorne

G. George I

H. Henry Hudson

I. Increase Mather

J. John Smith

K. James I

L. Robert Sieur de La Salle

N. Peter Minuit

O. Oliver Cromwell

P. Powhatan

Q. Elizabeth I

R. Roger Williams

S. Squanto

T. John Rolfe

U. Peter Stuyvesant

V. Virginia Date

W. John Winthrop

Map Identification: Use the map below to locate the following places:

Plymouth Colony	Massachusetts	Rhode Island
New Amsterdam	Pennsylvania	Maryland
Virginia	Carolina	Barbados
Antigua	Jamaica	Aruba

MULTIPLE CHOICE ANSWERS:

1. A	6. E	11. B	16. A
2. A	7. D	12. B	17. E
3. D	8. C	13. C	
4. A	9. B	14. D	
5. D	10. B	15. D	

CHRONOLOGICAL ARRANGEMENT ANSWERS:

James I becomes king of England

First Africans arrive in Jamestown

Plymouth Colony founded

Puritans found Massachusetts Bay

Williams/Hutchinson banished

English Civil War

Charles II restored to English throne

Carolina founded

New Netherland becomes New York

Pennsylvania founded

MATCHING ANSWERS:

1. K
2. L
3. U
4. J
5. P
6. T
7. B
8. O
9. S
10. W
11. R
12. A
13. N

3
A Meeting of Cultures

KEY TOPICS

✓ **Relations between European newcomers and native peoples**
✓ **Relations between Europeans and Africans**
✓ **Labor in the New World**

CHAPTER OUTLINE

I. Indians and Europeans
    A. Indian Workers in the Spanish Borderlands
    B. The Web of Trade
    C. Displacing Native Americans in the English Colonies
        1. Land use and property rights
        2. Colonial land acquisition
    D. Bringing Christianity to Native Peoples
        1. Catholic missionaries in Spanish colonies
        2. French Jesuits in Canada
        3. Missionaries in English colonies
    E. After the First Hundred Years: Conflict and War
        1. King Philip's War
        2. Bacon's Rebellion
        3. The Pueblo Revolt
        4. Resumption of the Beaver Wars

II. Africans and Europeans
    A. Labor Needs and the Turn to Slavery
    B. The Shock of Enslavement
    C. African Slaves in the New World
        1. Slavery in the southern colonies
        2. Slavery in the northern colonies
        3. Changing race relations in the colonies
        4. Repressive laws and slave codes
    D. African American Families and Communities
        1. The rise of the creole slave population
        2. Work and family life
        3. Community life and religion
    E. Resistance and Rebellion

III. European Laborers in Early America
    A. A Spectrum of Control
    B. New European Immigrants

IV. Conclusion

SELF-TESTING

Multiple Choice: In the blanks below, write the letter of the BEST response.

1. _____ According to the narrative of his life, Olaudah Equiano was at one time all of the following EXCEPT
   a. the son of an Igbo chief.
   b. a world traveler.
   c. the servant of a naval officer.
   d. a slave until the day he died.

2. _____ An Indian tribe's relationship with European newcomers depended upon
   a. population numbers.
   b. the intentions of the white immigrants.
   c. the various responses of the natives themselves.
   d. All of these factors are correct.

3. _____ Of all the groups of incoming Europeans, the group that strove most intently to enslave Native Americans were the
   a. Portuguese.
   b. Spanish.
   c. French.
   d. Dutch.
   e. English.

4. _____ Of all the groups of incoming Europeans, the group that most clearly understood native peoples and their concept of trade were the
   a. Portuguese.
   b. Spanish.
   c. French.
   d. Dutch.
   e. English.

5. _____ Consequence(s) of the trade relationship between Europeans and Native Americans ultimately included
   a. dependence of Native Americans on European manufactured goods.
   b. Europeans adopting native crafts.
   c. a decrease in hunting.
   d. All of these answers are correct.

6. _____ The "Beaver Wars" involved a struggle between the
   a. Iroquois and Hurons.
   b. Cherokees and Catawbas.
   c. Cherokees and Shawnees.
   d. Cheyennes and Shoshonis.
   e. Lakotas and Pawnees.

7. _____ Native Americans made use of all the lands they considered to belong to their tribe, even if that land appeared to be "vacant."
   a. True
   b. False

8. _____ Some white settlers obtained Indian land by
    a. fraud.
    b. buying from individuals who had no right to sell it.
    c. "right of conquest" following a war.
    d. simply settling on the land and then appealing to colonial governments for assistance.
    e. All of these means were employed.

9. _____ French Jesuit missionaries were more successful than their Spanish Franciscan counterparts in converting native peoples because of all the following reasons EXCEPT
    a. their approach was gradual and less confrontational.
    b. they demonstrated more sensitivity to Native traditions.
    c. they encouraged merchants to trade only with Christian Indians.
    d. their use of shame and guilt to convert native peoples.

10. _____ Which of the following did NOT involve Europeans fighting native peoples?
    a. King Philip's War
    b. King William's War
    c. Bacon's Rebellion
    d. The Pueblo Revolt.

11. _____ Most Africans forced into slavery in the Americas labored in the southern United States.
    a. True
    b. False

12. _____ In the New World, Europeans found that
    a. land was cheap and labor was expensive.
    b. land was expensive and labor was cheap.
    c. both land and labor were expensive.
    d. both land and labor were cheap.

13. _____ Typically, the enslavement of Native Americans failed because
    a. native men refused to perform agricultural labor, which they considered women's work.
    b. Indians, more familiar with the land, could escape and hide easily.
    c. disease and hard conditions depleted native populations.
    d. All of these reasons contributed to the failure.

14. _____ The term "Middle Passage" referred to the
    a. horrific trans-Atlantic crossing endured by Africans bound for a life of slavery in the Americas.
    b. newly discovered Appalachian opening at the Cumberland Gap.
    c. second leg of the triangular trade route between England, the Caribbean, and the northern colonies.
    d. well-traveled road between Philadelphia and Jamestown.

15. _____ In eighteenth-century Virginia, slaves eventually replaced white indentured servants as the primary source of cheap labor because
    a. willing white workers became harder to find.
    b. men and women could give planters a self-reproducing labor force.
    c. it was easier to recapture runaway blacks than runaway white indentured servants.
    d. slaves would never be the competitors of planters as former servants often were.
    e. All of these reasons contributed to this replacement.

16. _____ Slaves in the northern colonies would most likely be found
    a. on large New England farms.
    b. in small fishing villages.
    c. working in urban settings and occupations.
    d. intermarried with whites or Indians.

17. _____ Despite the brutality of slavery, creoles managed to create a form of normal family and community life because
    a. creoles enjoyed longer life spans than African-born slaves.
    b. creole women usually bore more children.
    c. young creoles grew up with no personal memories of Africa.
    d. ethnic or regional differences became less important.
    e. All of these factors helped creoles maintain a normal life.

18. _____ Which of the following was most often the LEAST successful method employed by African slaves to express their resistance to their plight?
    a. organized rebellion
    b. working slowly
    c. breaking tools
    d. pretending to be ill
    e. damaging property

19. _____ Most Europeans who immigrated to the colonies under the redemptioner system came from
    a. Germany.
    b. the Netherlands.
    c. Italy.
    d. England.
    e. Protestant France.

20. _____ Most groups of later (eighteenth-century) immigrants from Europe tended to settle in
    a. New England.
    b. the Chesapeake area.
    c. the coastal areas of South Carolina and Georgia.
    d. the foothills of the Appalachians.

Chronological Arrangement: Re-arrange the list of events below by **re-writing** each item in correct chronological sequence into the blanks provided.

Bacon's Rebellion in Virginia _____

Georgia established _____

Pequot War in New England _____

"King William's War" _____

"King Philip's War" _____

Slavery legalized in Georgia _____

First Africans arrive in Jamestown_____

Stono Rebellion in South Carolina_____

Scots-Irish begin coming to America_____

Portugal begins enslaving Africans_____

Essay: Read each of the following questions, take some time to organize your thoughts, then compose thorough, meaningful answers for each.

1. Explain the systems used by Spanish colonizers to force Native Americans to work for them.

2. How did concepts of land ownership and use differ between Native Americans and Europeans?

3. Compare and contrast Spanish, French, and English efforts to spread Christianity.

4. Explain why white American colonists turned to slavery as the answer to their labor needs.

5. Describe the process of enslavement—from Africa through the "Middle Passage" to the auction block in the Americas.

6. Describe the techniques used by African slaves to retain a semblance of normal family and community life.

7. In what ways were newer white European immigrants employed to work for those already there?

8. Describe Mary Rowlandson's time spent among the Indians of New England.

Matching: Match each description in the left column with the person it most likely describes. (Beware: Not all names will be used!)

1. _____ Son of an Igbo chief, survived the Middle Passage; saved enough money to buy his own freedom.

2. _____ French monarch whose invasion of the Rhineland sparked German emigration to America and Russia.

3. _____ Captured during King Philip's War, she published an account of her adjustment to Native Life.

4. _____ Puritan Minister who established "praying towns" where Indians could receive Christian training.

5. _____ Son of Massasoit; tired of white incursion and injustice, led a fierce insurrection in the 1670s.

6. _____ Frontier Virginian who led a violent rebellion against Indians *and* the colonial aristocracy.

7. _____ Led a temporarily successful Pueblo revolt against Spaniards and their Catholicism.

8. _____ Intended for his Georgia to be a refuge for English debtors, free from the "stain of slavery."

A. Popé

B. Nathaniel Bacon

C. Cotton Mather

D. John Davenport

E. John Eliot

F. John Folwell

G. George II

H. Henry Navarre

I. Increase Mather

J. James Oglethorpe

K. King Philip

L. Louis XIV

M. Mary Rowlandson

N. Olaudah Equiano

MULTIPLE CHOICE ANSWERS:

1. D	6. A	11. B	16. C
2. D	7. A	12. A	17. E
3. B	8. E	13. D	18. A
4. C	9. D	14. A	19. A
5. A	10. B	15. E	20. D

CHRONOLOGICAL ARRANGEMENT ANSWERS:

Portugal begins enslaving Africans

First Africans arrive in Jamestown

Pequot War in New England

"King Philip's War"

Bacon's Rebellion in Virginia

"King William's War"

Scots-Irish begin coming to America

Georgia established

Stono Rebellion in South Carolina

Slavery legalized in Georgia

MATCHING ANSWERS:

1. N
2. L
3. M
4. E
5. K
6. B
7. P
8. J

4

English Colonies in an Age of Empire

KEY TOPICS

- ✓ **The Function of the Colonies within the British Empire**
- ✓ **Maturing Colonial Life and Lifestyles**
- ✓ **The Colonies and the Clash of European Empires**

CHAPTER OUTLINE

I. Economic Development and Imperial Trade in the British Colonies
    A. The Regulation of Trade
    B. The Colonial Export Trade and the Spirit of Enterprise
    C. The Import Trade and Ties of Credit
    D. Becoming More Like England: The Growth of Cities and Inequality
        1. Artisans in colonial cities
        2. The growing gap between rich and poor

II. The Transformation of Culture
    A. Goods and Houses
    B. Shaping Minds and Manners
    C. Colonial Religion and the Great Awakening

III. The Colonial Political World
    A. The Dominion of New England and the Limits of British Control
    B. The Legacy of the Glorious Revolution
    C. Diverging Politics in the Colonies and Great Britain

IV. Expanding Empires
    A. British Colonists in the Backcountry
    B. The Spanish in Texas and California
    C. The French along the Mississippi and in Louisiana

V. A Century of Warfare
    A. Imperial Conflict and the Establishment of an American Balance of Power, 1689–1738
    B. King George's War Shifts the Balance, 1739–1754
    C. The French and Indian War, 1754–1760: A Decisive Victory
    D. The Triumph of the British Empire, 1763

VI. Conclusion

SELF-TESTING

Multiple Choice: In the blanks below, write the letter of the BEST response.

1. _____ According to the text, the chief ambition of the young George Washington was to
   a. be a professional soldier.
   b. be a famous surveyor.
   c. hold political office.
   d. cut down fewer cherry trees.
   e. live as a proper English country gentleman.

2. _____ To England, the colonies' most important function within the Empire was to
   a. supply raw materials.
   b. purchase goods manufactured in England.
   c. become self-sufficient as quickly as possible.
   d. all of these functions.
   e. Only a and b are correct.

3. _____ The concept of mercantilism involved
   a. building national power.
   b. achieving a favorable balance of trade.
   c. exporting more than importing.
   d. colonies.
   e. All of these factors were involved.

4. _____ Products that were required to be funneled through England before going to or from the colonies were called
   a. enumerated.
   b. subsidized.
   c. contraband.
   d. fortunate.

5. _____ During the colonial period, the southern colonies exported large quantities of all of the following EXCEPT
   a. rice.
   b. indigo.
   c. cotton.
   d. tobacco.
   e. naval stores.

6. _____ Colonial New England's most important economic activity involved
   a. large scale farming.
   b. the sea.
   c. manufacturing.
   d. all of these activities.
   e. Only a and b are correct.

7. _____ Most colonial artisans worked
   a. in small local factories.
   b. in large regional factories.
   c. in workshops attached to houses.
   d. on the estates of southern aristocrats.

8. _____ Generally, American colonists
   a. experienced less poverty than their English counterparts.
   b. enjoyed a higher standard of living than their English counterparts.
   c. had access to available land.
   d. All of these answers are correct.
   e. Only a and c are correct.

9. _____ According to the text, the majority of eighteenth-century American colonists
   a. strove to live the lifestyles of the English elite.
   b. readily altered their belief to match the latest European trends.
   c. imported a few European household goods.
   d. lived in grand, multi-roomed homes.

10. _____ The highest levels of literacy in Colonial America could be found
    a. in New England.
    b. in the Chesapeake.
    c. in the South.
    d. on the frontier.

11. _____ Colonial intellectuals never gained acceptance by or the affirmation of their English counterparts.
    a. True
    b. False

12. _____ The prevailing thought of the Enlightenment said that
    a. the universe operated according to natural laws.
    b. humans gained knowledge and understanding through divine revelation.
    c. God continually directed human history.
    d. God had no role in the creation of the universe.

13. _____ In 1662, New England clergymen adopted the Halfway Covenant, which
    a. required prospective members to give evidence of their spiritual conversion.
    b. allowed baptized (but unconverted) adults to have their own children baptized.
    c. released non-members from having to pay taxes to support the Congregationalist Church.
    d. created a compromise between Calvinism and Arminianism.

14. _____ Among colonial regions, the Anglican Church was strongest in
    a. New England.
    b. the Middle Colonies.
    c. the South.
    d. the Frontier.

15. ____ Although the colonies were spiritually diverse, the eighteenth-century religious phenomenon that united them with each other and with England was
   a. Deism.
   b. the Enlightenment.
   c. the Great Awakening.
   d. the beginnings of Methodism.

16. ____ According to the text, as a result of revivals, colonial churches often experienced splits between
   a. New Lights and Old Lights.
   b. Enthusiasts and Traditionalists.
   c. Calvinists and Arminianists.
   d. clergy and laity.

17. ____ By emphasizing freedom of choice and resistance to authority, the Great Awakening laid part of the philosophical foundation for the coming American Revolution.
   a. True
   b. False

18. ____ The first attempt to unify multiple colonies into a single administrative unit was known as
   a. the Glorious Revolution.
   b. mercantilism.
   c. the Dominion of New England.
   d. the Albany Plan of Union.

19. ____ During the eighteenth century, colonists began to view as their most legitimate authority
   a. governors appointed and sent by the monarch.
   b. the House of Lords.
   c. Councils appointed and sent by the monarch.
   d. the House of Commons.
   e. locally elected colonial assemblies.

20. ____ British America had
   a. economic elites but no aristocracy.
   b. a natural, elitist aristocracy.
   c. a titled nobility.
   d. neither an elite class nor a titled aristocracy.

21. ____ The notion that all members of Parliament adequately could represent the interests of all Englishmen everywhere was known as
   a. actual representation.
   b. a unitary form of government.
   c. nonsense.
   d. virtual representation.

22. ____ Most colonists in the "backcountry"
    a. lived a crude lifestyle.
    b. were small, subsistence farmers.
    c. inhabited the foothills of the Appalachians.
    d. were newer English, Scots-Irish, or German immigrants.
    e. were all of these.

23. ____ The most significant of the Anglo-French wars in the early-eighteenth century was
    a. King William's War.
    b. Queen Anne's War.
    c. King George's War.
    d. the French and Indian War.

24. ____ The Native American group who tried to maintain neutrality between England and France was the
    a. Pequots.
    b. Powhatan Confederacy.
    c. Iroquois.
    d. Choctaw/Chickasaw Confederation.

25. ____ The French and Indian (Seven Years') War was fought in
    a. North America.
    b. the Caribbean.
    c. Asia.
    d. all of these places.

26. ____ In the Treaty of Paris (1763), that ended the French and Indian (Seven Years') War, France lost
    a. every possession in the western hemisphere.
    b. North America but retained its Caribbean possessions.
    c. only the territory between the Appalachians and the Mississippi. River, retaining the area known as "Louisiana."
    d. territory south of the Great Lakes but retained Canada.

27. ____ The Anglican minister Charles Woodmason found residents of the colonial backcountry all of the following EXCEPT
    a. "less than interested" in his preaching.
    b. extremely ignorant.
    c. spiritually flourishing.
    d. mostly illiterate.

Chronological Arrangement: Re-arrange the list of events below by **re-writing** each item in correct chronological sequence into the blanks provided.

James II becomes King of England _____

"King William's" War   _____

Seven Years' War   _____

Great Awakening begins   _____

Charles II becomes King of England _____

"King George's" War   _____

"Queen Anne's" War   _____

First Navigation Acts enacted   _____

England's Glorious Revolution   _____

Salem Witch Trials   _____

Essay: Read each of the following questions, take some time to organize your thoughts, then compose thorough, meaningful answers for each.

1. Explain the economic theory called "mercantilism." How did colonies contribute to the concept?

2. Why did England enact the Navigation Acts? What was the difference between enumerated and subsidized products?

3. Discuss economics and lifestyles within America's cities. Why were they more like English provincial towns than colonial villages?

4. In what cultural ways did well-to-do colonists strive to emulate the English aristocracy?

5. What was the Enlightenment? In what ways did the movement shape American activity?

6. What was the Great Awakening? In what ways did shifting theology unite—and divide—American colonists and their mother country?

7. Why was there a "Glorious Revolution"? How did that bloodless coup affect the American colonies?

8. What was the "backcountry"? How did life there differ from those of the east coast?

9. Why were Spain and France beginning their control in the New World in the eighteenth century?

10. How were native peoples affected by the series of struggles between England and France?

11. In what ways were colonial life changed by the British victory over the French and the Treaty of Paris in 1763?

Matching: Match each description in the left column with the person it most likely describes. (Beware: Not all names will be used!)

1. _____ His explanation of gravity suggested that humans could discover the natural laws of the universe.

2. _____ Member of the Royal Society, he invented the lightening rod, bifocals, and an iron stove.

3. _____ Anglican minister who toured the colonies after 1739 with a charismatic evangelistic style.

4. _____ Monarch who viewed colonies only as land and prizes to award to patrons.

5. _____ Monarch whose conversion to Catholicism sparked the Glorious Revolution.

6. _____ Aristocratic governor of the Dominion of New England whose rule antagonized colonists.

7. _____ Would-be country squire who surrendered to French forces from Ft. Duquesne.

8. _____ Congregationalist minister who led revival in Massachusetts; he railed at parishioners sinfulness

9. _____ Ingenious British War Minister who decided to give colonists more say in prosecuting the war.

10. _____ English minister disgusted by the crudity of life in the colonial backcountry.

A. Edmund Andros

B. Edward Braddock

C. Charles II

D. James Davenport

E. Jonathan Edwards

F. Benjamin Franklin

G. George Whitefield

H. Alexander Hamilton

I. Isaac Newton

J. James II

K. Bathsheba Kingsley

L. Mother Ann Lee

M. Charles Woodmason

N. George Washington

O. William of Orange

P. William Pitt

Map Identification: Use the maps on the following page to show the changes made by the Seven Years' War and the subsequent Treaty of Paris. Locate these features:

British Territory	Major British Cities
French Territory	Major French Cities
Spanish Territory	Ft. Duquesne (Ft. Pitt)

North America **before** 1763:

North America **after** 1763:

MULTIPLE CHOICE ANSWERS:

1. E	10. A	19. E
2. E	11. B	20. A
3. E	12. A	21. D
4. A	13. B	22. E
5. C	14. C	23. D
6. B	15. C	24. C
7. C	16. A	25. D
8. D	17. A	26. B
9. C	18. C	27. C

CHRONOLOGICAL ARRANGEMENT ANSWERS:

First Navigation Acts enacted

Charles II becomes King of England

James II becomes King of England

England's Glorious Revolution

"King William's" War, Salem Witch Trials

"Queen Anne's" War

Great Awakening begins

"King George's" War

Seven Years' War

MATCHING ANSWERS:

1. I
2. F
3. G
4. C
5. J
6. A
7. N
8. E
9. P
10. M

5
Imperial Breakdown

KEY TOPICS

- ✓ **Changes in British Philosophy and Empire Administration**
- ✓ **Reactions in the Colonies**
- ✓ **Steps on the Road to Revolution**

CHAPTER OUTLINE

I. Imperial Reorganization
    A.   British Problems
    B.   Dealing with the New Territories
    C.   The Status of Native Americans
    D.   Curbing the Assemblies
    E.   The Sugar and Stamp Acts

II. American Reactions
    A.   Constitutional Issues
    B.   Taxation and the Political Culture
    C.   Protesting the Taxes

III. The Aftermath of the Stamp Act Crisis
    A.   A Strained Relationship
    B.   Regulator Movements

IV. The Townshend Crisis
    A.   Townshend's Plan
    B.   American Boycott
    C.   The Boston Massacre
    D.   The "Quiet Period"
    E.   The Boston Tea Party
    F.   The Intolerable Acts

V. The Road to Revolution
    A.   Protestantism and the American Response to the Intolerable Acts
    B.   The First Continental Congress
    C.   The Continental Association
    D.   Political Divisions

VI. Conclusion

SELF-TESTING

Multiple Choice: In the blanks below, write the letter of the **best** response.

1. ____ Before the French and Indian War, the American colonists had paid no direct British taxes.
   a. True
   b. False

2. ____ British problems in North America after 1763 included all of the following EXCEPT
   a. a smallpox epidemic.
   b. Indian populations likely to be resentful or hostile.
   c. autonomous colonial assemblies.
   d. an enormous national debt as a result of the war.

3. ____ Compared to the average Englishman, most colonists paid
   a. an equal percentage of taxes.
   b. an inordinately large share of the tax burden.
   c. only a fraction of the tax percentages.
   d. a slightly smaller share of tax.

4. ____ The unpopular Proclamation of 1763 was intended to
   a. prohibit white settlement west of the Appalachians.
   b. keep white settlers and Native People apart.
   c. contain colonists closer to the coast where they could be more easily controlled.
   d. accomplish all of these goals.

5. ____ During the French and Indian War, the Cherokees had
   a. fought on the side of the French.
   b. fought alongside the British.
   c. managed to remain neutral.
   d. switched allegiance as the war progressed.

6. ____ The first direct or "internal" tax placed upon the American colonists was contained in the
   a. Sugar Act.
   b. Stamp Act.
   c. Townshend Duties.
   d. Tea Act.
   e. Declaratory Act.

7. ____ The British Constitution was (and is)
   a. housed, along with the Crown Jewels, in the Tower of London.
   b. only a collection of British law and custom.
   c. written in Latin and, therefore, inaccessible to most Britons.
   d. protected, along with the Magna Carta, in the British Museum.

8. _____ "Country ideology" believed (and believes) that
   a. a standing army is a threat to personal liberty.
   b. large governments are not to be trusted.
   c. local governments are more responsive than remote ones.
   d. executive power must be checked and balanced.
   e. All of these notions were country ideology.

9. _____ Colonists objected to Parliament taxing them because they saw it as unconstitutional.
   a. True
   b. False

10. _____ Which of the following was NOT a colonial idea?
    a. the Albany Congress
    b. the Stamp Act Congress
    c. Committees of Correspondence
    d. the First Continental Congress

11. _____ Probably the most effective weapon used by the colonists to protest taxation was
    a. vigilante activity aimed at British agents.
    b. boycotting British merchants.
    c. official demonstrations enacted by colonial congresses.
    d. threats of armed revolution.

12. _____ Regulators engaged in
    a. clock making.
    b. vigilante activities in the Carolinas.
    c. efforts to promote colonial unification.
    d. smuggling to evade British customs agents.

13. _____ Although Parliament repealed most of the Townshend Duties, to restate the right to tax the colonies, they retained the sole tax on
    a. paint.
    b. liquor.
    c. paper documents.
    d. sugar.
    e. tea.

14. _____ The Coercive Acts
    a. completely closed the port of Boston.
    b. allowed a British official accused of killing a colonist to be tried in England.
    c. limited the number of town meetings in Massachusetts.
    d. did all of these things.

15. _____ The Quebec Act did all of the following EXCEPT
    a. extend Canadian jurisdiction south to the Ohio River.
    b. infringe upon the western lands claimed by Connecticut, Pennsylvania, and Virginia.
    c. deprive would-be settlers of their prospective homesteads on the frontier.
    d. limit the spread of Catholicism along the frontier.

16. ____ By 1774, mostly because of the "Intolerable Acts," a majority of colonists now favored independence from Britain.
    a. True
    b. False

Chronological Arrangement: Re-arrange the list of events below by **re-writing** each item in correct chronological sequence into the blanks provided.

Parliament passes Sugar Act   _____

Boston Massacre   _____

First Continental Congress meets   _____

American Revolution begins   _____

Peace of Paris (1763)   _____

Townshend Duties imposed   _____

Coercive Acts passed   _____

French and Indian War begins   _____

Gaspee burned   _____

Stamp Act imposed   _____

Essay: Read each of the following questions, take some time to organize your thoughts, then compose thorough, meaningful answers for each.

1. List and discuss the factors that prompted the change in British colonial policy after the French and Indian War.

2. Why did the British government have a problem with colonial assemblies? How did they attempt to limit their influence?

3. Why and how did Native Americans' ability to protect themselves diminish after 1763?

4. Define "country ideology." How did this concept drive a wedge between the British government and its North American colonies?

5. List and describe the process whereby thirteen separate colonies began to unite in common cause against England.

6. Discuss the methods employed by American colonists to protest British taxation.

7. How did the Quebec Act frighten colonists and lead to further strain and alienation?

8. How did British "Salutary Neglect" (Chapter 4) contribute to the reluctance of the Americans to accept British rule following 1763? Was the Revolution a product of British tyranny or lack of wisdom?

9. What did the "Mechanicks" of South Carolina have to say to the condescending William Henry Dayton?

Matching: Match each description in the left column with the person it most likely describes. (Beware: Not all names will be used. Some may be used **twice**!)

1. _____ Ottawa chief who led a coalition of eight Native tribes against the northern British frontier in 1763.

2. _____ Appeared before Parliament to present American objections to the Sugar and Stamp Acts.

3. _____ Political philosopher who justified revolution if government exceeds protecting the public good.

4. _____ Prime Minister who began the shift from regulating colonial commerce to direct internal taxation.

5. _____ Virginia lawyer whose strong resolutions against the Stamp Act were published throughout America.

6. _____ Boston merchant whose arrest for smuggling led to a riot, then to the stationing of British troops.

7. _____ British Prime Minister (1770–1782) who, in 1770, was prepared to concede that the Townshend duties had been counterproductive.

8. _____ Killed in the Boston Massacre, he was called "that half Indian, half negro and altogether rowdy".

9. _____ Boston leader of the Sons of Liberty; a speech of his likely incited the Boston Tea Party.

10. _____ British general in charge of Boston; quartering his troops wherever he wanted inflamed Bostonians.

11. _____ South Carolina aristocrat who needed a reminder that artisans and merchants are people too.

A. Samuel Adams

B. Benjamin Franklin

C. Crispus Attucks

D. William Henry Drayton

E. Thomas Gage

F. Eliza Farmer

G. George Grenville

H. Patrick Henry

I. Pasquale Paoli

J. John Hancock

K. George III

L. John Locke

M. Massasoit

N. Lord North

O. James Otis

P. Pontiac

Q. Anne Stuart

R. Edmund Randolph

MULTIPLE CHOICE ANSWERS:

1. A
2. A
3. C
4. D
5. B
6. B
7. B
8. E
9. A

10. A
11. B
12. B
13. E
14. D
15. D
16. B

CHRONOLOGICAL ARRANGEMENT ANSWERS:

French and Indian War begins

Peace of Paris

Parliament passes Sugar Act, Stamp Act imposed

Townshend Duties imposed

Boston Massacre

Gaspee burned

Coercive Acts passed

First Continental Congress meets

American Revolution begins

MATCHING ANSWERS:

1. P
2. B
3. L
4. G
5. H
6. J
7. N
8. C
9. A
10. E
11. D

6
The War for Independence

KEY TOPICS

- ✓ **The Beginning of the Revolutionary War**
- ✓ **Three Phases and their Major Battles**
- ✓ **The War's Outcome**

CHAPTER OUTLINE

I.   The Outbreak of War and the Declaration of Independence, 1774–1776
- A.   Mounting Tensions
- B.   The Loyalists' Dilemma
- C.   British Coercion and Conciliation
- D.   The Battles of Lexington and Concord
- E.   The Second Continental Congress, 1775–1776
- F.   Commander-in-Chief George Washington
- G.   Early Fighting: Massachusetts, Virginia, the Carolinas, and Canada
- H.   Independence
- I.   Religion, Virtue, and Republicanism

II. The Combatants
- A.   Professional Soldiers
- B.   Women in the Contending Armies
- C.   African-American Participation in the War
- D.   Native Americans and the War

III. The War in the North, 1776–1777
- A.   Britain Hesitates: Crucial Battles in New York and New Jersey
- B.   The Year of the Hangman: Victory at Saratoga and Winter at Valley Forge

IV. The War Widens, 1778–1781
- A.   The United States Gains an Ally
- B.   Fighting on the Frontier and at Sea
- C.   The Land War Moves South
- D.   American Counterattacks

V.   The American Victory, 1782–1783
- A.   The Peace of Paris
- B.   The Components of Success

VI. War and Society, 1775–1783
- A.   The Women's War
- B.   Effect of the War on African Americans
- C.   The War's Impact on Native Americans

SELF-TESTING

Multiple Choice: In the blanks below, write the letter of the BEST response.

1. _____   When Britain made Thomas Gage (a military general) governor of Massachusetts, the people of that colony
   a. formed a Committee of Safety.
   b. began stockpiling weapons.
   c. began organizing a volunteer militia.
   d. did all of these.

2. _____   At the beginning of armed hostilities, the percentage of American colonists who claimed loyalty to England was about
   a. 10 percent.
   b. 20 percent.
   c. 50 percent.
   d. 70 percent.

3. _____   The British government under Prime Minister Lord North never tried to reach an amicable compromise with the American colonists.
   a. True
   b. False

4. _____   When they convened in 1775, the Second Continental Congress did all of the following EXCEPT
   a. create a Continental Army and authorize a navy.
   b. establish a Post Office.
   c. appoint a Bostonian to command the new army.
   d. authorize the printing of paper money.
   e. extend a peace proposal to George III.

5. _____   According to the text, George Washington was ideal for the position as Commander in Chief of the Continental Army because he
   a. had never lost a military campaign.
   b. was a highly trained, professional soldier.
   c. was blessed with good judgment and the gift of command.
   d. was confident in his ability to do the job.
   e. All of these answers are correct.

6. _____   The British ultimately abandoned Boston because
   a. of their staggering losses at Breed's (Bunker) Hill.
   b. Washington occupied high ground, placing them in a precarious position.
   c. Thomas Gage's Boston wife convinced him to do so.
   d. there was no armed opposition in the city.
   e. Only b and d are correct.

7. ____ According to John Locke (and others), the "contract" theory of government states that
   a. rulers are God's chosen representatives on earth.
   b. a ruler can and should come to power by any means possible, even those that are violent or unscrupulous.
   c. legitimate government rests on an agreement between the people and their rulers, and exists only as long as the rulers offer them protection.
   d. monarchy is one of three branches of government, the others being aristocracy and democracy.

8. ____ Which of the following is NOT a component of the Declaration of Independence?
   a. an opening statement explaining the purpose of the document
   b. an assumption that people have natural rights
   c. the premise that governments exist to safeguard natural rights
   d. a list of specific charges, proving that British government had violated its reason for being
   e. a tentative framework of government creating a provisional legislature

9. ____ Those who supported "republicanism"
   a. were related to the proponents of "country ideology."
   b. called for government by consent of the governed.
   c. were suspicious of excessively centralized government.
   d. believed in the need for a virtuous, public-spirited citizenry.
   e. All of these are a part of "republicanism."

10. ____ The American Revolution was won by
    a. colonial militias.
    b. sturdy, patriotic citizen-soldiers.
    c. a distrusted but needed professional army.
    d. embattled farmers.

11. ____ Among the woman who often accompanied the Continental Army were all of the following EXCEPT
    a. prostitutes.
    b. wives and mistresses of officers.
    c. wives and mistresses of ordinary soldiers.
    d. recruits who had been promised farms by the Continental Congress.
    e. cooks and nurses.

12. ____ Because of fears of arming them, no African Americans actively fought on either side during the American Revolution.
    a. True
    b. False

13. ____ During the Revolutionary War, it was in native peoples' best interest to side with the
    a. British.
    b. colonists.
    c. French.
    d. Spanish.

14. _____ According to the text, during the first phase of the Revolution, Britain attempted to solidify loyalist support in the South.
   a. suppress a mainly New England revolt.
   b. cut off New England from the rest of the colonies.
   c. accomplish all of these goals.
   d. Only b and c are correct.

15. _____ Britain's New York strategy failed because
   a. Burgoyne's advance was slowed by baggage and terrain.
   b. Howe became distracted by trying to finish off Washington.
   c. Burgoyne's reinforcements failed to arrive to help at Saratoga.
   d. All of these factors had a part in the failed strategy.

16. _____ France ultimately decided to aid the Americans because
   a. of the victory at Saratoga.
   b. it believed the United States might have a viable future.
   c. it hoped to get back at its old nemesis England.
   d. it wanted to avoid possible reversals of fortune.
   e. All of these are correct.

17. _____ France was alone in opposing Britain in the War.
   a. True
   b. False

18. _____ A "frigate" is a
   a. warship.
   b. musical instrument.
   c. water conductor.
   d. Franklin invention.
   e. None of these answers are correct.

19. _____ Lord Cornwallis had to surrender at Yorktown on October 19, 1781 because
   a. he became trapped on the York Peninsula.
   b. he could not be reinforced quickly enough.
   c. the French fleet had cut off all possibility of evacuating his army.
   d. all of these answers.
   e. Only a and b are correct.

20. _____ In the Peace of Paris (1783), the United States secured its independence plus territory
   a. westward to the Appalachians.
   b. westward to the Mississippi River.
   c. westward to the Rocky Mountains.
   d. northward to Hudson's Bay (Canada).

21. _____ During the Revolution, American women
   a. assumed more responsibilities at home.
   b. assumed more public roles.
   c. supported the war effort directly.
   d. supported the war effort indirectly.
   e. did all of these.

22. ____ Most Europeans were never affected by the Americans' war, thought of it as simply a passing anomaly, and saw no greater meaning in the outcome.
   a. True
   b. False

Chronological Arrangement: Re-arrange the list of events below by *re-writing* each item in correct chronological sequence into the blanks provided.

Hessians surprised at Trenton _____

Americans win at Saratoga _____

Declaration of Independence signed_____

Cornwallis surrenders at Yorktown_____

Peace of Paris (1783) _____

Battles of Lexington, Concord _____

Brutal winter at Valley Forge _____

Battle of Breed's (Bunker) Hill _____

Battle of Cowpens _____

Paine publishes *Common Sense* _____

Essay: Read each of the following questions, take some time to organize your thoughts, then compose thorough, meaningful answers for each.

1. In what ways did the decisions and actions of British politicians aggravate and alienate American colonists?

2. Why did the Second Continental Congress appoint George Washington as Commander in Chief of the Continental Army?

3. What were Thomas Jefferson and the other drafters of the Declaration of Independence trying to accomplish?

4. Discuss "republicanism." How is it related to "country ideology"?

5. How did the war affect women? African Americans? Native Americans?

7. How did the New York campaign and the resulting Battle of Saratoga lead to the alliance with France?

8. Why was the war in the South bloodier than the "civilized" warfare experienced in the North?

9. History is often "what happened," but it is also often what people convince themselves **must** have happened. Why did (and have) Americans convinced themselves that the Revolution was won by local militias of "citizen soldiers" like the "Minutemen"?

Matching: Match each description in the left column with the person it most likely describes. (Beware: Not all names will be used. Some may be used **twice**!)

1. British commander, military governor of Massachusetts; tried to confiscate arms at Concord

    A. Thomas Paine

2. Prime minister whose hard line against Boston inflamed anti-British sentiment

    B. William Howe

3. Reluctant Virginia soldier; realized that American independence depended upon a professional army

    C. Benedict Arnold

4. English corset maker whose radical ideas (including independence) were published in *Common Sense*

    D. George Washington

5. English philosopher whose contract theory underlays the writing of the Declaration of Independence

    E. Horatio Gates

6. Once complained that republicanism was a shadowy concept to define

    F. Abigail Adams

7. British commander in chief in New York who became preoccupied with catching Washington

    G. John Locke

8. General who led Americans to victory at Saratoga

    H. Thomas Gage

9. Along with John Adams and John Jay in Paris, masterfully concluded the Peace of Paris (1783)

    I. Lord North

10. Author of the Declaration of Independence and diplomat to England in 1786

    J. Thomas Jefferson

11. Woman who wrote "Remember the Ladies"

    K. George III

    L. John Adams

    M. Benjamin Franklin

Matching: Match each Revolutionary War Battle listed in the left column with the outcome listed in the right column.

1. ____ Lexington

2. ____ Breed's Hill ("Bunker Hill")

3. ____ Brooklyn Heights

4. ____ Trenton

5. ____ Saratoga

6. ____ Kaskaskia

7. ____ Charleston, S.C.

8. ____ Camden, S.C.

9. ____ Guilford Court House

10. ____ Yorktown

A. American victory

B. British victory

C. Contested/Indecisive

Map Identification: Use the map below to locate each of the battles listed in the Matching section above.

MULTIPLE CHOICE ANSWERS:

1. D	10. C	19. D
2. B	11. D	20. B
3. B	12. B	21. E
4. C	13. A	22. B
5. C	14. E	
6. B	15. D	
7. C	16. E	
8. E	17. B	
9. E	18. A	

CHRONOLOGICAL ARRANGEMENT ANSWERS:

Battle of Lexington

Concord; Battle of Breed's (Bunker) Hill

Paine publishes *Common Sense*

Declaration of Independence signed

Hessians surprised at Trenton

Americans win at Saratoga

Brutal winter at Valley Forge

Battle of Cowpens

Cornwallis surrenders at Yorktown

Peace of Paris (1783)

MATCHING ANSWERS:

1. H	
2. I	
3. D	
4. A	
5. G	
6. L	
7. B	
8. E	
9. M	
10. J	
11. F	

MATCHING ANSWERS:

1. C	
2. C	
3. B	
4. A	
5. A	
6. A	
7. B	
8. B	
9. C	
10. A	

7
The First Republic

KEY TOPICS

- ✓ **A Plethora of Post-War Problems**
- ✓ **The Articles of Confederation**
- ✓ **The Constitution**

CHAPTER NOTES

I. The New Order of Republicanism
   A. Defining the People
   B. Women and the Revolution
      1. The Revolution and African Americans in the South
      2. Northern Blacks and the Revolution
      3. The Revolution's impact on Native Americans
   C. The State Constitutions
      1. Toward religious pluralism
      2. Conflicting visions of republicanism
   D. The Articles of Confederation

II. Problems at Home
   A. The Fiscal Crisis
   B. Economic Depression
   C. The Economic Policies of the States
      1. Shays's Rebellion
      2. Debtors vs. conservatives
   D. Congress and the West

III. Diplomatic Weaknesses
   A. Impasse with Britain
   B. Spain and the Mississippi River

IV. Toward a New Union
   A. The Road to Philadelphia
   B. The Convention at Work
      1. The Great Compromise
      2. Regulation of commerce and the issue of slavery
      3. The office of the chief executive
   C. Overview of the Constitution
   D. The Struggle over Ratification

V. Conclusion

SELF-TESTING

Multiple Choice: In the blanks below, write the letter of the BEST response.

1.____   In the years immediately following the end of the Revolution, most American government power was to be found in
   a.   the newly ratified Articles of Confederation.
   b.   the constitutions and legislatures of state governments.
   c.   the old Continental Congress.
   d.   none of these places.

2.____   To most Americans, "republicanism" meant that
   a.   political power lies with the people.
   b.   people elect officials who represent their interests.
   c.   people should define and limit government power.
   d.   All of these answers are correct.

3.____   For American women, the Revolution brought
   a.   a reversal of their limited rights and privileges.
   b.   no gains in rights whatsoever.
   c.   limited gains in their rights.
   d.   substantial and revolutionary advancements.

4.____   The percentage of African Americans who had gained their freedom by the end of the war was about
   a.   3 percent.
   b.   10 percent.
   c.   25 percent.
   d.   40 percent.

5.____   Most white Americans in the new northern states
   a.   viewed slavery as incompatible with the ideals of the Revolution.
   b.   pushed for immediate emancipation.
   c.   still displayed racial prejudice.
   d.   all of these are correct.
   e.   Only a and c are correct.

6.____   Following the Revolution, most Native Americans
   a.   were happy to be part of the new United States.
   b.   viewed themselves as citizens only of their own nations.
   c.   were interested in full participation in state and national government.
   d.   wanted independence.
   e.   Only b and d are correct.

7.____   The citizens of most of the new states thought that the British concept of "constitution" (a collection of evolving customs and practices) was a good idea.
   a.   True
   b.   False

8.____   To make state governments more expressive of the will of the people, most state constitutions provided

    a. lower property requirements for voting.
    b. annual election of officials.
    c. increased numbers of seats in legislatures.
    d. bicameral legislatures independent of the executive.
    e. all of these innovations.

9.____   According to the text, the most important thing lacking under the Articles of Confederation was

    a. a national chief executive.
    b. a national judiciary.
    c. the congress' power to tax.
    d. a bill of rights.

10. ____   In the years immediately following the Revolutionary War, the new American economy experienced

    a. a depression.
    b. a clash between debtors and creditors.
    c. the closing of British markets to American goods.
    d. a national government powerless to make significant changes.
    e. all of these situations.

11. ____   Those who rebelled along with Daniel Shays in 1786 were mostly

    a. backcountry southern farmers angry with east coast aristocrats over unchecked Indian raids.
    b. Massachusetts farmers worried about foreclosure and debtors imprisonment.
    c. backcountry Pennsylvanians who didn't want to pay taxes.
    d. southern slaveholders protesting possible abolition.

12. ____   The most significant successes of the Confederation Congress lay in

    a. settling problems in the West.
    b. handling tricky foreign affairs.
    c. steering clear of entangling foreign alliances.
    d. easing the nation's financial malaise.

13. ____   The Land Ordinance of 1785 provided for the orderly division of western land into townships of _____ uniform sections of _____ acres each.

    a. 10; 40
    b. 10; 80
    c. 36; 640
    d. 640; 1,000

14. ____   The Northwest Ordinance of 1787

    a. provided an orderly method whereby a region could become a territory, then a state.
    b. stipulated that the area north of the Ohio River should become three, four, or five new states.
    c. said that a territory could become a state when its adult, male population reached 60,000.
    d. barred slavery from the Northwest Territory.
    e. provided all of these.

15. ____ Following the American Revolution, Britain did all of the following EXCEPT
   a. considered its former colonies to be valuable trading partners.
   b. became upset over the post-war treatment of Loyalists.
   c. retained its troublesome series of forts around the Great Lakes.
   d. tried to lure Vermont into an alliance.
   e. tried to play one sovereign state against another.

16. ____ During the 1780s, Spain proved to be a valuable and dependable ally in securing United States sovereignty and prestige.
   a. True
   b. False

17. ____ The biggest dilemma faced by the Constitution writers in Philadelphia concerned
   a. whether to include a powerful chief executive office.
   b. property requirements for political participation.
   c. how states and their populations should be represented in the new Congress.
   d. what toppings to order on their pizzas.

18. ____ In the Constitution, southern states increased their representation in Congress by
   a. annexing western territories.
   b. counting every five slaves as three persons.
   c. rejecting the New Jersey Plan.
   d. threatening to secede and then ally with Spain.

19. ____ The Philadelphia delegates envisioned an "electoral college" which would
   a. eliminate popular or congressional election of the president.
   b. insulate the president from the whims of an uninformed public and the intrigues of the legislature.
   c. allow the president to be checked by an independent regulatory body.
   d. create "red states" and "blue states."

20. ____ The framers of the Constitution assumed that America's citizenry always would act
   a. nobly, as true believers in the republican principle.
   b. from disinterested virtue.
   c. in the best interest of the public.
   d. out of considerations of self-interest.

21. ____ So "ambition [could] counter ambition," the framers provided all of the following EXCEPT:
   a. an effective standing army.
   b. counterbalanced blocs of power.
   c. an internal system of checks and balances.
   d. federalism.

22. ____ According to the text, the fears and concerns of anti-federalists were assuaged by
   a. a promised bill of rights.
   b. Madison, Jay, and Hamilton in *The Federalist*.
   c. the notion that they could have both an empire and personal freedom.
   d. all of these factors.

Chronological Arrangement: Re-arrange the list of events below by **re-writing** each item in correct chronological sequence into the blanks provided.

Land Ordinance of 1785 _____

The Federalist _____

Declaration of Independence signed_____

Articles of Confederation proposed_____

Constitution ratified into effect _____

Shay's Rebellion _____

Treaty of Paris ends the Revolution_____

Northwest Ordinance _____

Philadelphia Constitutional Convention _____

Post-war Depression begins _____

Essay: Read each of the following questions, take some time to organize your thoughts, then compose thorough, meaningful answers for each.

1. How and why did different Americans define "the people" differently in the period following the Revolutionary War?

2. How were post-war African Americans treated in the South? In the North?

3. What ideas and assumptions did citizens write into their state constitutions?

4. Discuss government under the Articles of Confederation. Why was it ineffective?

5. List and describe the factors that led to economic collapse in the decade following the war.

6. Describe and illustrate relations between the United States and Britain after the Revolution.

7. How did relations with Spain affect post-war expansion in the Southwest?

8. What were some of the main issues the delegates grappled with at the Philadelphia Convention? How were they resolved?

9. List and discuss some of the major differences between the Articles of Confederation and the Constitution of 1787.

10. How was the society of the new United States viewed by the French traveler St. John Crevecoeur?

Who Said It: Match each quote in the left column with the person who most likely said it or the document from which it is most likely taken. (Note: They may be used **more than once** or **not at all**.)

1. _____ "We hold these Truths to be self-evident; That all men are created equal, That they are endowed by their Creator with certain unalienable Rights; That among these are Life, Liberty, and the Pursuit of Happiness. . ."

2. _____ "Each state retains its sovereignty, freedom, and independence, and every power, jurisdiction, and right . . ."

3. _____ ". . . That to secure these Rights, Governments are instituted among Men, deriving their just Powers from the Consent of the Governed . . ."

4. _____ "In determining questions in the United States in Congress assembled, each State shall have one vote."

5. _____ " . . . That whenever any Government becomes destructive of these ends, it is the Right of the People to alter or abolish it . . ."

6. _____ "We the People of the United States, in order to form a more perfect union, establish justice, insure domestic tranquility, provide for the common defense, promote the general welfare, and secure the blessings of liberty to ourselves and our posterity . . ."

7. _____ "Here are no aristocratical families, no courts, no kings, no bishops, no ecclesiastical dominion, no invisible power giving to a very few . . . no great manufactures employing thousands, no great refinements of luxury . . ."

8. _____ "The executive power shall be vested in a President of the United States of America."

9. _____ "Congress shall make no law respecting an establishment of religion or prohibiting the free exercise thereof . . ."

A. John Adams

B. *Bill of Rights*

C. *Constitution*

D. *Declaration of Independence*

E. St. John Crevecoeur

F. *The Federalist*

G. George Washington

H. Patrick Henry

I. Articles of Confederation

MULTIPLE CHOICE ANSWERS:

1. B
2. D
3. C
4. B
5. E
6. E
7. B
8. E
9. C
10. E
11. B
12. A
13. C
14. E
15. A
16. B
17. C
18. B
19. B
20. D
21. A
22. D

CHRONOLOGICAL ARRANGEMENT ANSWERS:

Declaration of Independence signed

Articles of Confederation proposed

Treaty of Paris ends the Revolution

Post-war depression begins

Land Ordinance of 1785

Shays's Rebellion

Philadelphia Constitutional Convention

Northwest Ordinance

The Federalist

Constitution ratified into effect

WHO SAID IT? ANSWERS:

1. D
2. I
3. D
4. I
5. D
6. C
7. E
8. C
9. B

8

A New Republic and the Rise of Parties

KEY TOPICS

- ✓ **Life in the New United States**
- ✓ **Launching an Experiment in Government**
- ✓ **The Federalist Era: High Tide and Decline**

CHAPTER OUTLINE

  I.   Washington's America
      A.   The Uniformity of New England
      B.   The Pluralism of the Mid-Atlantic Region
      C.   The Slave South and Its Backcountry
      D.   The Growing West

  II.   Forging a New Government
      A.   "Mr. President" and the Bill of Rights
      B.   Departments and Courts
      C.   Revenue and Trade
      D.   Hamilton and the Public Credit
      E.   Reaction and Opposition

  III.   The Emergence of Parties
      A.   The French Revolution
           1.   Franco-American relations
           2.   The growth of Democratic-Republican societies
      B.   Securing the Frontier
      C.   The Whiskey Rebellion
      D.   Treaties with Britain and Spain
      E.   The First Partisan Election

  IV.   The Last Federalist Administration
      A.   The French Crisis and the XYZ Affair
      B.   Crisis at Home
      C.   The End of the Federalists

  V.   Conclusion

SELF-TESTING

Multiple Choice: In the blanks below, write the letter of the BEST response.

1. _____ By March 4, 1789, most members of the government under the new Constitution seemed eager to get started.
   a. True
   b. False

2. _____ As the new nation began, probably the most socially, ethnically, and theologically homogenous region was
   a. New England.
   b. the middle states.
   c. the southern states.
   d. the new western states.

3. _____ During the 1780s, many southerners, animated by the ideals of the Revolution
   a. questioned the morality of slavery.
   b. freed their own slaves.
   c. feared competition from freed blacks.
   d. experienced all of these.
   e. experienced none of these.

4. _____ Many planters' sons, limited in the land they could obtain in the established southern states
   a. abandoned agriculture and migrated to the North to start factories.
   b. abandoned agriculture and started businesses in southern cities.
   c. bought neighbors' lands at skyrocketing prices.
   d. migrated to the West to start new plantations.

5. _____ One of the first debates in the new Congress centered upon
   a. where to locate the new capital city.
   b. maintaining free navigation of the Mississippi River.
   c. how much they should be compensated for their services.
   d. what formal title should be used when addressing the president.
   e. the influence of lobbyists.

6. _____ To appease anti-federalists worried about a remote and dangerous system of national courts, Congress
   a. enacted the Judiciary Act of 1789.
   b. created a hierarchical system of state, district, and circuit courts.
   c. suggested the "nuclear option" to break filibusters.
   d. insisted on confirming the appointments of judicial appointees.

7. _____ Alexander Hamilton's comprehensive financial plan called for
   a. the federal assumption of all states' debts at par.
   b. an excise tax on whiskey.
   c. the chartering of a national bank.
   d. interregional economic dependence, unified by manufacturing.
   e. all of these measures.

8. _____ Those who launched an armed rebellion against Hamilton's ideas in 1794 were mostly
   a. backcountry southern farmers angry with east coast aristocrats over unchecked Indian raids.
   b. Massachusetts farmers worried about foreclosure and debtors imprisonment.
   c. backcountry Pennsylvanians who didn't want to pay tax on distilled liquor.
   d. southern slaveholders protesting possible abolition.

9. _____ Jay's Treaty accomplished all of the following EXCEPT
   a. stopping the British practice of impressment.
   b. getting the British to abandon their string of forts in the old Northwest.
   c. getting the British to open trade opportunities in India and the Caribbean.
   d. granting the British "most favored nation" status.

10. _____ According to the text, the first "partisan election" was that of
    a. 1792 (Washington and Jefferson).
    b. 1796 (Adams and Jefferson).
    c. 1800 (Adams and Jefferson).
    d. 1884 (Blaine and Tilden).
    e. 2000 (Bush and Gore).

11. _____ The French foreign ministers who demanded a bribe and a hefty American loan for the privilege of talking to them were known as
    a. the Jacobins.
    b. the Directory.
    c. the Triumvirate.
    d. René, Etienne, and Maurice.
    e. X, Y, and Z.

12. _____ The four misguided, questionably constitutional, and politically ruinous laws passed by congressional Federalists in 1798 were called collectively
    a. Direct Tax.
    b. Hamilton's Financial Plan.
    c. the Alien and Sedition Acts.
    d. the Kentucky and Virginia Resolutions.

13. _____ The first state to introduce the doctrine known as "nullification" was
    a. Tennessee.
    b. Kentucky.
    c. Vermont.
    d. Virginia.
    e. South Carolina.

14. _____ Federalists seemed to seal their political fate when they
    a. passed Hamilton's financial program.
    b. nominated Adams for a second term in 1800.
    c. began using a powerful military to squelch opposition.
    d. asked Congress to declare war on France.

15. _____ The philosophy known as Deism
    a. was an outgrowth of the eighteenth-century Enlightenment.
    b. suggested that God did create the universe, but only as an impersonal force.
    c. rejected divine revelation in favor of human reason.
    d. alarmed many orthodox American clerics.
    e. was all of these.

Chronological Arrangement: Re-arrange the list of events below by **re-writing** each item in correct chronological sequence into the blanks provided.

Bill of Rights added to the Constitution _____

Whiskey Rebellion suppressed   _____

Jefferson elected   _____

XYZ Affair   _____

Constitution ratified into effect   _____

Pinckney's Treaty with Spain   _____

Citizen Genêt angers Washington _____

Washington's first Inauguration   _____

Jay's Treaty with Britain   _____

Louis XVI executed in France   _____

Essay: Read each of the following questions, take some time to organize your thoughts, then compose thorough, meaningful answers for each.

1. Discuss the urgent problems faced by the nation as the new Constitution went into effect.

2. Compare and contrast New England society with that of the mid-Atlantic states in 1790.

3. What was Alexander Hamilton trying to accomplish—specifically and generally—with his comprehensive financial program?

4. What were the grounds of Republican worries and opposition to Hamilton's financial plan?

5. Why did the United States draw close to war with France in the 1790s?

6. Characterize and discuss the presidential election of 1796. What was unique about the outcome?

7. Why did the Federalists enact the controversial Alien and Sedition Acts? What was the Republican response?

8. Though John Adams is usually not considered one of America's great presidents, to his credit he forestalled trouble abroad and at home. How did he accomplish this, and at what cost to him politically?

9. List and discuss the factors that began the demise of the Federalist Party.

Matching: Match each description in the left column with the person it most likely describes. (Beware: Not all names will be used. Some may be used **more than once**!)

1. _____ Only president elected unanimously

2. _____ Secretary of the Constitutional Convention, he became an early, forceful leader in the House.

3. _____ First Secretary of the Treasury

4. _____ Along with Madison, gave the name Republican to the party that opposed the Federalists.

5. _____ French ambassador; ignored Washington's wish to remain neutral.

6. _____ Revolutionary War hero who subdued Ohio Indians at the Battle of Fallen Timbers.

7. _____ A *Federalist* author; first Chief Justice; arranged a controversial treaty with Britain.

8. _____ His "Farewell Address" warned Americans about political parties and entangling foreign alliances.

9. _____ Federalist victor in 1796; President during the, XYZ affair; his patience and willingness to negotiate kept the United States out of war.

10. _____ German auctioneer; leading a Pennsylvania revolt led to his conviction for treason.

11. _____ Second Vice President; opposed Hamilton; defeated Adams (and Burr) for president in 1800.

A. John Adams

B. Aaron Burr

C. Charles C. Pinkney

D. Thomas Jefferson

E. Edmond Genêt

F. John Fries

G. George Washington

H. Alexander Hamilton

I. Increase Mather

J. John Jay

K. Don Diego de Gardoqui

L. Little Turtle

M. James Madison

N. "Mad" Anthony Wayne

O. James Otis

P. Thomas Paine

Matching: Match each description or characteristic in the left column with the group most likely to reflect it.

1. ____ New England   A. Federalist

2. ____ Backcountry/the West   B. Anti-federalist/Republican

3. ____ Followers of Thomas Jefferson

4. ____ Agreed with Alexander Hamilton

5. ____ Admired the French Revolution

6. ____ Horrified by the French Revolution

Map Identification: In the map below, locate each of these nations of Native People's traditional homeland:

Iroquois	Miamis	Shawnees
Catawbas	Cherokees	Creeks
Wyandots	Ottawas	Kickapoos
Winnebagos	Potawatomis	Seminoles

MULTIPLE CHOICE ANSWERS:

1. B
2. A
3. D
4. D
5. D
6. A
7. E
8. C
9. A

10. B
11. E
12. C
13. B
14. C
15. E

CHRONOLOGICAL ARRANGEMENT ANSWERS:

Constitution ratified into effect

Washington's first Inauguration

Louis XVI executed in France

Bill of Rights added to the Constitution

Citizen Genêt angers Washington

Whiskey Rebellion suppressed

Jay's Treaty with Britain

Pinckney's Treaty with Spain

XYZ Affair

Jefferson elected

MATCHING ANSWERS:

1. G
2. M
3. H
4. D
5. E
6. N
7. J
8. G
9. A
10. F
11. D

MATCHING ANSWERS:

1. A
2. B
3. B
4. A
5. B
6. A

9

The Triumph and Collapse of Jeffersonian Republicanism

KEY TOPICS

- ✓ **Jefferson's Successes and Problems**
- ✓ **The War of 1812 and its Aftermath**
- ✓ **The "Era of Good Feelings"**

CHAPTER OUTLINE

I. Jefferson's Presidency
   - A. Reform at Home
   - B. The Louisiana Purchase
   - C. Florida and Western Schemes
   - D. Embargo and a Crippled Presidency

II. Madison and the Coming of War
   - A. The Failure of Economic Sanctions
   - B. The Frontier and Indian Resistance
   - C. Decision for War

III. The War of 1812
   - A. Setbacks in Canada
   - B. Western Victories and British Offensives
   - C. The Treaty of Ghent and the Battle of New Orleans

IV. The Era of Good Feelings
   - A. Economic Nationalism
   - B. Judicial Nationalism
   - C. Toward a Continental Empire

V. The Breakdown of Unity
   - A. The Panic of 1819
   - B. The Missouri Compromise
   - C. The Election of 1824

VI. Conclusion

SELF-TESTING

Multiple Choice: In the blanks below, write the letter of the BEST response.

1. _____ As president, Thomas Jefferson wanted
   a. to continue the ideals and legacy of the Revolution.
   b. to create and ensure an agrarian republic.
   c. additional land for American yeoman farmers.
   d. All of these are correct.

2. _____ Jefferson's delegation to France was authorized to buy
   a. New Orleans.
   b. a thirty-year lease of the port of New Orleans.
   c. the Louisiana Territory from the Gulf of Mexico to Canada and westward to the Rocky Mountains.
   d. legally secured navigation rights on the Mississippi River.
   e. All of these are correct.

3. _____ The Louisiana Purchase accomplished all of the following EXCEPT
   a. more than doubling the size of the national domain.
   b. buying more than 800,000 square miles for less than 4 cents per acre.
   c. forcing the United States into a military alliance with France.
   d. requiring the idealist Jefferson to become more pragmatic.
   e. requiring the strict constructionist Jefferson to use the implied powers of the Constitution.

4. _____ On the pretense of returning runaway sailors, Britain engaged in
   a. purchasing slaves once again from Africa.
   b. impressment of sailors from the decks of American ships.
   c. expanding its empire into the Far East for an additional workforce.
   d. allowing women to travel on board naval vessels.

5. _____ The most flagrant violation by the British of American navigation was the
   a. Tecumseh uprising.
   b. abrogation of Jay's Treaty.
   c. *Chesapeake* Incident.
   d. rescinding of the Orders in Council.

6. _____ Those most hurt by Jefferson's Embargo Act were
   a. American shippers.
   b. American manufacturers.
   c. British merchants.
   d. Napoleon's huge army.

7. _____ The United States declared war on Britain in 1812 because of
   a. continued impressments of American sailors.
   b. the apparent incitement and arming of the Tecumseh uprising.
   c. the War Hawks' desire to invade and keep Canada and Florida.
   d. All of these factors led to the declaration of war.

8. _____ All of the following are true about the War of 1812 EXCEPT
   a. It was a debacle, for the most part, for the American army.
   b. The war had overwhelming support of Congress.
   c. The war was a cause for deep divisions of Americans along party, sectional, and religious lines.
   d. It was strongly supported in the South and the West.

9. _____ According to the text, the Battle of New Orleans was an anti-climax to a war that had already ended.
   a. True
   b. False

10. _____ What was the experience of Native Americans in the war?
    a. They refused to take sides at all.
    b. They experienced relatively low battle casualties, compared to others later in American history.
    c. The number of Native Americans who fought and died in the Battle of New Orleans was the largest in the history of American-Indian warfare.
    d. Their loyalty won them the admiration of Andrew Jackson.

11. _____ As the result of their war opposition and the rhetoric at their ill-timed Hartford Convention, the _____ Party suffered an irreversible blow to their reputation and national power.
    a. Republican
    b. Democrat
    c. Federalist
    d. Whig

12. _____ The Era of Good Feelings (1815–1824) witnessed all of the following EXCEPT
    a. temporary political harmony and sectional unity.
    b. a surge of national pride and patriotism.
    c. the lack of any major, divisive issues.
    d. the emergence of a new generation of political leadership.
    e. a president running unopposed for re-election.

13. _____ Calhoun's (and others') economic nationalism included calls for
    a. a re-chartered national bank.
    b. the first protective tariff.
    c. funds earmarked for internal improvements.
    d. All of these are correct.

14. _____ Which of the following cases led to the strongest statement supporting national power over the states?
    a. *Marbury v. Madison*
    b. *McCulloch v. Maryland*
    c. *Fletcher v. Peck*
    d. *Dartmouth College v. Woodward*

15. _____ In the Trans-Continental (Adams/Onís) Treaty of 1819
    a. The United States annexed Florida.
    b. Spain renounced claim to the Oregon Territory.
    c. The United States renounced its claim to Texas.
    d. The United states assumed $5 million of Spanish debts to American citizens.
    e. All of these were accomplished.

16. _____ The loss of Spanish colonies in the New World prompted the
    a. Missouri Compromise.
    b. Mexican War.
    c. Spanish-American War.
    d. Monroe Doctrine.

17. _____ The Missouri Compromise
    a. admitted Missouri as a slave state.
    b. admitted Maine as a separate free state.
    c. temporarily maintained a delicate free/slave state balance in the Senate.
    d. established a line above which all new states would be free of slavery.
    e. All of these are correct.

18. _____ The presidential election of 1824 was decided by
    a. the popular vote.
    b. the electoral college.
    c. the House of Representatives.
    d. a coin toss.

Chronological Arrangement: Rearrange the list of events below by **rewriting** each item in correct chronological sequence into the blanks provided.

Embargo Act passed by Congress _____

Burr kills Hamilton in a duel _____

Battle of New Orleans _____

Madison succeeds Jefferson _____

War of 1812 begins _____

Louisiana Purchase _____

Treaty of Ghent signed _____

"The Prophet" killed at Tippecanoe_____

Jefferson first inaugurated _____

Burr conspiracy revealed _____

Essay: Read each of the following questions, take some time to organize your thoughts, then compose thorough, meaningful answers for each.

1. What realities caused the idealist Thomas Jefferson to have to adjust his principles regarding naval strength and strict constructionism?

2. Discuss the influence of John Marshall upon the Supreme Court and upon the nation.

3. How did the West of Lewis and Clark differ from the West of today?

4. Discuss the bizarre public life of Aaron Burr.

5. Discuss the role played (or not played) by James Madison in the prelude to war with Britain.

6. How and why did the War of 1812 go so badly for the Americans?

7. What factors and events stimulated the period known as the "Era of Good Feelings"?

8. Describe the nationalistic economic proposals of John C. Calhoun and Henry Clay.

9. Why could John Quincy Adams be considered a link between the Puritans' "City on a Hill" and what would later be termed "Manifest Destiny"?

10. What was the purpose of the Monroe Doctrine? How was news of this statement likely received in the capitals of Europe?

11. Why did the question of Missouri statehood become such a problem? How was the problem resolved?

12. Discuss the reappearance of partisan politics as the Election of 1824 approached.

Matching: Match each description in the left column with the person it most likely describes. (Beware: Not all names will be used. Some may be used **more than once!**)

1. _____ Good fortune gave him an admirable first term, but his second was embroiled in controversy

2. _____ Federalist Chief Justice (1801-1834); established judicial review in *Marbury v. Madison*

3. _____ His plans for reviving a French empire got him Louisiana but went awry in Haiti

4. _____ Killed Hamilton in a duel,

5. _____ Jefferson's Secretary of State; later, the president who led the United States to war in 1812

6. _____ Renowned Shawnee orator who tried to create a pan-Indian movement to resist white encroachment

7. _____ American Commodore whose defeat of a British fleet led to control of the Great Lakes

8. _____ Tennessee planter; defeated hostile Creeks at Horseshoe Bend, then the British at New Orleans

9. _____ Madison's Secretary of State; elected president in 1816, then ran unopposed in 1820

10. _____ "War Hawk" from Kentucky; suggested a compromise on the Missouri issue

11. _____ Brilliant Secretary of State; his vision for America included a coast-to-coast empire

12. _____ Indian fighter; his 1818 invasion of Spanish Florida led to a Trans-Continental Treaty the next year

13. _____ His statement made the Western Hemisphere off-limits to further European colonization

14. _____ Opponents suggested that his election by the House was part of a "corrupt bargain"

A. John Adams

B. Aaron Burr

C. Henry Clay

D. James Madison

E. David Erskine

F. David Farragut

G. Christopher Gadsden

H. Alexander Hamilton

I. Isaac Watts

J. Thomas Jefferson

K. Francis Scott Key

L. Louis XVI

M. John Marshall

N. Napoleon

O. Oliver H. Perry

P. Zebulon Pike

Q. John Q. Adams

R. James Monroe

S. Roger Sherman

T. Tecumseh

U. Abel Upshur

V. Stephen Van Rensselaer

W. Andrew Jackson

Map Identification: In the map below, locate each of these items:

Maine
Lewis and Clark route
Tippecanoe
Oregon Territory

Spanish Florida
St. Louis
Put-In-Bay
Missouri Compromise Line

Louisiana Territory
New Orleans
Missouri

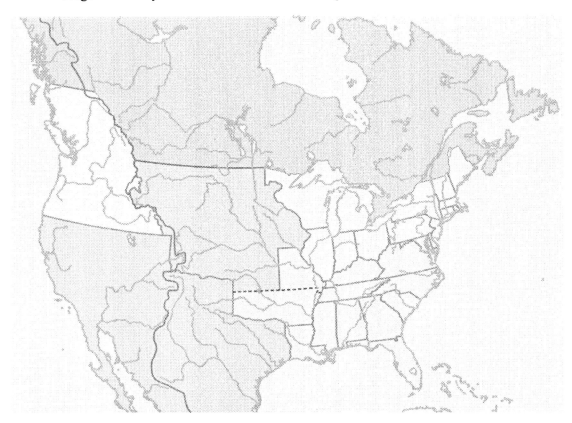

MULTIPLE CHOICE ANSWERS:

1. D
2. A
3. C
4. B
5. C
6. A
7. D
8. B
9. B
10. C

11. C
12. C
13. D
14. B
15. E
16. D
17. E
18. C

CHRONOLOGICAL ARRANGEMENT ANSWERS:

Jefferson first inaugurated

Louisiana Purchase

Burr kills Hamilton in a duel

Burr conspiracy revealed

Madison succeeds Jefferson

Embargo Act passed by Congress

"The Prophet" killed at Tippecanoe

War of 1812 begins

Treaty of Ghent signed

Battle of New Orleans

MATCHING ANSWERS:

1. J
2. M
3. N
4. B
5. D
6. T
7. O
8. W
9. R

10. C
11. Q
12. W
13. R
14. Q

10
The Jacksonian Era

KEY TOPICS

- ✓ **Changes in Democracy in America**
- ✓ **The Presidency of Jackson and His Successor**
- ✓ **The Whigs and the Second Party System**

CHAPTER OUTLINE

I.   The Egalitarian Impulse
    A.   The Extension of White Male Democracy
        1.   Extending the suffrage and democratic reform
        2.   The disfranchisement of free blacks and women
    B.   The Popular Religious Revolt
        1.   Evangelicalism and minority rights
        2.   The limits of equality
    C.   The Rise of the Jacksonians

II.   Jackson's Presidency
    A.   Jackson's Appeal
    B.   Indian Removal
    C.   The Nullification Crisis
    D.   The Bank War

III.   Van Buren and Hard Times
    A.   The Panic of 1837
    B.   The Independent Treasury
    C.   Uproar over Slavery

IV.   The Rise of the Whig Party
    A.   The Party Taking Shape
    B.   Whig Persuasion
    C.   The Election of 1840

V.   The Whigs in Power
    A.   Harrison and Tyler
    B.   The Texas Issue
    C.   The Election of 1844

VI.   Conclusion

SELF-TESTING

Multiple Choice: In the blanks below, write the letter of the BEST response.

1. _____ The "egalitarian impulse" was driven by all of the following EXCEPT
   a. the opening of politics to mass participation.
   b. evangelical religion.
   c. the rapid populating of the American frontier and "forest-born" democracy.
   d. the dominant Protestant churches.

2. _____ Between 1800 and 1850, regular church attendance
   a. declined dramatically due to the absence of organized religion on the frontier.
   b. increased dramatically due to the absence of traditional, elitist religion on the frontier.
   c. decreased somewhat due to the inaccessibility of churches in rural areas.
   d. increased dramatically due to the evangelical rejection of Calvinism and the emphasis on free salvation for all.
   e. Only b and d are correct.

3. _____ In the wake of the Second Great Awakening, American women
   a. found means of expression outside the political realm.
   b. were relegated to spectators in most religious services.
   c. began to assume positions of leadership in major denominations.
   d. began to lose interest in spiritual matters.

4. _____ In the presidential election of 1828
   a. the personalities of the candidates were more important than issues.
   b. voters perhaps chose "image over ideas" and "style over substance."
   c. voter turnout increased from 25% four years earlier to 55%.
   d. Democrats convinced voters that they were the people's champions against aristocracy, though many Democratic leaders were aristocrats too.
   e. all of these were characteristics.

5. _____ The system whereby a victorious party can give government jobs to its supporters and remove incumbent appointees from the opposition party is known as
   a. "politics as usual."
   b. "pork."
   c. the "spoils system."
   d. a "crying shame."
   e. the "American System."

6. _____ Which of the following did NOT constitute part of Henry Clay's American System?
   a. a protective tariff
   b. a national bank
   c. Federal subsidies for "internal improvements"
   d. Indian removal to supply additional room for southern agriculture
   e. an integrated—and unifying—national economy

7. ____ Which of the following nations of Native Americans was NOT removed to Indian Territory as a result of Jackson's forced removal policy?
   a. Choctaws
   b. Creeks
   c. Chickasaws
   d. Cherokees
   e. Cheyennes

8. ____ In the cases of *Cherokee Nation v. Georgia* and *Worcester v. Georgia*, John Marshall sided with the
   a. Jackson administration.
   b. state of Georgia.
   c. Cherokees.
   d. "Albany Regency."

9. ____ The Nullification Crisis involved
   a. tariff rates that favored the industrial North at the expense of the rural South.
   b. states' rights vs. federal pre-eminence.
   c. a personal feud between Andrew Jackson and John C. Calhoun.
   d. all of these issues.

10. ____ In response to the Whigs' use of the National Bank to trap him in 1832, Jackson
    a. allowed the bank to expire quietly four years later.
    b. fired Nicholas Biddle, the bank's president.
    c. set out vindictively to destroy the bank.
    d. surprised and trumped the Whigs' ploy by signing the bank's recharter.

11. ____ The Panic of 1837 and the resulting economic depression happened because
    a. money from the old national bank had been deposited in pet banks and then loaned to western land speculators.
    b. British demand for cotton dropped.
    c. worried investors rushed to redeem notes, only to discover that their banks had no hard currency (specie).
    d. of all of these factors.

12. ____ When northern abolitionists barraged the South with inflammatory literature, Jackson
    a. joined them in denouncing slavery as a moral outrage.
    b. denounced evangelical ministers as alarmists for creating a problem where there was none.
    c. approved when postmasters censored the mail.
    d. blamed the mounting tension on his old nemesis Henry Clay.

13. ____ The Anti-Mason Party was openly suspicious of
    a. the building profession.
    b. evangelical religion.
    c. the Order of Freemasons.
    d. defense attorneys.

14. ____ To capture the presidency in 1836, the new Whig Party
    a. nominated Henry Clay, who had failed to defeat Jackson but who perhaps had a better chance against Van Buren.
    b. ran several regional candidates.
    c. tried to force the election into the House of Representatives.
    d. did all of these.
    e. Only b and c are correct.

15. ____ As president, John Tyler's philosophy was one of agrarian states'-rights pitted him against the urban and commercial elements of the Whig party.
    a. True
    b. False

16. ____ Regarding the annexation of Texas, all of the following statements are true EXCEPT
    a. Most of Texas lies south of the Missouri Compromise line and would become, therefore, one or more slave states.
    b. Jackson believed the annexation of Texas might trigger war with Mexico.
    c. Texans themselves wished to remain independent.
    d. John C. Calhoun thought that the security and preservation of the Union demanded the annexation of Texas.

17. ____ To win the support of skeptical northerners, Texas' annexation was ultimately linked to that of
    a. the abolition of slavery.
    b. the annexation of Oregon.
    c. tariff reduction.
    d. economic recovery.
    e. all of these factors.

18. ____ The president who finally annexed Texas was
    a. Jackson.
    b. Van Buren.
    c. Harrison.
    d. Tyler.
    e. Polk.

19. ____ The heritage of the Jackson era in the political realm included
    a. highlighting the presidency as the focal point of American politics.
    b. mastering the art of tailoring issues and especially images to reach wide audiences.
    c. the diffusing of sectional tension through party competition.
    d. All of these are correct.
    e. Only a and b are correct.

Chronological Arrangement: Re-arrange the list of events below by **re-writing** each item in correct chronological sequence into the blanks provided.

First publication of the *Liberator* _____

Texas War for Independence _____

Andrew Jackson first elected _____

Texas admitted to the Union _____

Harrison's 32-day presidency _____

Jackson vetoes the Bank _____

Panic of 1837 _____

The "corrupt bargain" _____

Compromise tariff diffuses
nullification _____

Indian Removal Act _____

Essay: Read each of the following questions, take some time to organize your thoughts, then compose thorough, meaningful answers for each.

1. In your opinion, was Andrew Jackson the *initiator* or the *beneficiary* of the democratic reforms and innovations of the 1820s? Explain.

2. In your opinion, was the Democratic Party of the 1830s truly the party of the "common man," or was this merely a carefully cultivated image?

3. List and discuss the ways American politics became more "egalitarian" in the first three decades of the nineteenth century.

4. What was the theological message and popular appeal of the Second Great Awakening? How did this coincide with the democratizing of American politics?

5. In what ways did the presidential campaign of 1828 differ from those of the present day?

6. Describe the process that led to the Cherokees' infamous "Trail of Tears."

7. What was the "Eaton Affair"? What impact did this seemingly minor thing have on the relationship between South Carolina and the United States?

8. Discuss the events that led from the attempted rechartering of the Second National Bank to the Panic of 1837.

9. Why were the Whigs able to emerge as the winners of the Election of 1840?

10. Why was the Election of 1844 a referendum on westward expansion?

Matching: Match each description or characteristic in the left column with the group most likely to reflect it.

1. _____ New England	A. Democrat	
2. _____ The West	B. Whig	
3. _____ The South	C. Both parties	
4. _____ Congregationalists		
5. _____ Methodists and Baptists		
6. _____ Defenders of Americans' liberties		
7. _____ Favored the National Bank		
8. _____ Favored easy credit for speculative ventures		
9. _____ Blamed for the Panic of 1837		
10. _____ Accused of playing to the class envy of the poor		
11. _____ Led by congressional opponents of Jackson		
12. _____ Absorbed the Anti-Masons		
13. _____ Bankers, manufacturers, small-businessmen		
14. _____ Subsistence farmers, unskilled workers		
15. _____ Scots-Irish, Irish, and German Catholics		
16. _____ John C. Calhoun		
17. _____ Martin Van Buren		
18. _____ Henry Clay		
19. _____ Daniel Webster		
20. _____ James Knox Polk		

MULTIPLE CHOICE ANSWERS:

1. D	11. D
2. E	12. C
3. A	13. C
4. E	14. E
5. C	15. A
6. D	16. C
7. E	17. B
8. C	18. D
9. D	19. D
10. C	

CHRONOLOGICAL ARRANGEMENT ANSWERS:

The "corrupt bargain"

Andrew Jackson first elected

Indian Removal Act

First publication of the *Liberator*

Jackson vetoes the Bank

Compromise tariff diffuses nullification

Texas War for Independence

Panic of 1837

Harrison's 32-day presidency

Texas admitted to the Union

MATCHING ANSWERS:

1. B
2. A
3. A
4. B
5. B
6. C
7. B
8. A
9. A
10. A
11. B
12. B
13. A
14. A
15. A
16. B
17. A
18. B
19. B
20. A

11
Slavery and the Old South

KEY TOPICS

✓ **Regional Variations with the Old South**
✓ **The Life and Sub-culture of Slaves, Free Blacks, and Whites**

CHAPTER OUTLINE

I. The Lower South
 A. Cotton and Slaves
 B. The Profits of Slavery
  1. The slave trade
  2. Urban Slavery
  3. Industrial Slavery

II. The Upper South
 A. A Period of Economic Adjustment
  1. Growing urbanization
 B. The Decline of Slavery

III. Slave Life and Culture
 A. Work Routines and Living Conditions
  1. Diet and housing
  2. Working conditions
 B. Families and Religion
 C. Resistance

IV. Free Society
 A. The Slaveholding Minority
  2. Planters' wives
  3. Small slaveholders
 B. The White Majority
 C. Free Black People

V. The Proslavery Argument
 A. Religious Arguments
 B. Racial Arguments

VI. Conclusion

SELF-TESTING

Multiple Choice: In the blanks below, write the letter of the BEST response.

1. _____ According to the text, slavery
   a. made the South distinctive.
   b. was the foundation of personal fortunes.
   c. was the basis for social standing and mobility.
   d. served as the means of racial control.
   e. was all of these.

2. _____ Cotton became "king" in the Lower South because
   a. tobacco had lost its profitability.
   b. the perfecting of the cotton gin made it commercially attractive.
   c. it required less initial start-up capital than sugar or rice.
   d. that region had a long growing season, adequate rainfall, and fertile soil.
   e. of all of these factors.

3. _____ One of the reasons slavery became linked as an indispensable part of cotton production was because
   a. it required fairly continuous tending throughout the year, thus maximizing the return on capital invested in slave labor.
   b. it was easier for slaves to work with as compared to corn.
   c. Both of these answers are correct.
   d. Neither of these answers are correct.

4. _____ In the early nineteenth century, the greatest demand for southern cotton came from
   a. British textile mills.
   b. France.
   c. the North.
   d. southern textile mills.
   e. the German states.

5. _____ The price of a slave in the South in the early nineteenth century depended upon
   a. the age, sex, and health of the slave.
   b. which region of the South the sale took place.
   c. what skills the slave might have.
   d. the age of female slaves.
   e. all of these factors.

6. _____ Most slaveholders sought to avoid industrialization because
   a. cotton was too profitable to switch.
   b. planters considered free factory workers to be potential abolitionists.
   c. factory working slaves would often act too "independent."
   d. All of these answers are correct.
   e. Only a and c are correct.

7. _____ As tobacco and cotton land in the older states wore out through overuse, most southern farmers before 1850
   a. sold their land and moved west.
   b. experimented with alternative crops.
   c. practiced more progressive agricultural techniques.
   d. hired on former slaves as factory workers.

8. _____ The Upper South retained an economic stake in slavery because
   a. agricultural diversification made slavery profitable again.
   b. they sold slaves to the Lower South.
   c. wheat growing was labor-intensive.
   d. they were shifting to an industrial economy.
   e. slaves were cheaper to own than immigrant workers were to pay.

9. _____ Most slaves sought to retain vestiges of dignity through all of the following EXCEPT
   a. family and kinship ties.
   b. religious beliefs.
   c. frequent, violent uprisings.
   d. trying to individualize their cabins.
   e. subtle forms of resistance and subversion.

10. _____ Most "slave codes" prohibited
   a. property ownership.
   b. leaving the plantation without written permission.
   c. slaves' testimony against whites in court.
   d. teaching slaves to read and write.
   e. All of these were prohibited.

11. _____ Most slaves worked and acted out of
   a. affection toward their owners.
   b. pride in jobs well-done.
   c. lucrative work incentives.
   d. *esprit de corps*
   e. fear.

12. _____ Slaves on small farms experienced all of the following EXCEPT
   a. closer contact with the master's family.
   b. more direct exposure to the whims of their owners.
   c. more varied and less taxing workloads.
   d. a greater opportunity to live in complete family units.
   e. a greater likelihood of being sold if the masters' financial situation declined.

13. _____ Most religious expression among slaves derived
   a. directly from specific African traditions they had brought with them.
   b. from regular Christian education on most plantations.
   c. from a patchwork of common African traditions mingled with Christianity.
   d. from the evangelical message of spiritual equality and its confirmation of personal worth.
   e. Only c and d only correct.

14. _____ Which of these rebellions was ultimately successful?
   a. Gabriel Prosser's Rebellion (1800)
   b. Denmark Vessey's Conspiracy (1822)
   c. Nat Turner's Rebellion (1831)
   d. All of these rebellions were successful.
   e. None of these rebellions were successful.

15. _____ The best place for runaway slaves to retain their freedom was
   a. Pennsylvania, because of its Quaker heritage.
   b. Massachusetts, because of the many transcendentalists there.
   c. Illinois, because most farmers there would hide them.
   d. Canada, because the Fugitive Slave Law didn't apply there.

16. _____ Most planters lived in opulent, feudal splendor in large houses.
   a. True
   b. False

17. _____ Free blacks in the South
   a. had to carry papers proving they were indeed free.
   b. could not demonstrate upward mobility.
   c. were shut out of legal and political systems.
   d. tended to work as farm laborers or tenants.
   e. were all of these.

18. _____ To justify slavery to northerners (and to themselves), southerners
   a. cited biblical proof texts to argue that slavery was part of God's plan.
   b. asserted that slaves were better treated than "wage slaves" in the North.
   c. argued that blacks were unfit for freedom among white people.
   d. presumed that moral chaos would be the result of emancipation.
   e. employed all of these.

19. _____ . Most whites in the North were less racist than their northern counterparts.
   a. True
   b. False

20. _____ By 1850, planters in the Lower South
   a. realized that slavery was immoral.
   b. were fearful of the increase in plantations in the Upper South, and saw them as competition.
   c. believed the only solution to their dilemma was to become a separate nation.
   d. saw that cotton had no future, and contemplated turning to tobacco as a major crop.

Chronological Arrangement: Rearrange the list of events below by rewriting each item in correct chronological sequence into the blanks provided.

Hinton Helper's *Impending Crisis* _____

Denmark Vessey's Conspiracy _____

First slaves arrive at Jamestown _____

Florida/Texas admitted to the Union_____

Eli Whitney patents the Cotton Gin_____

Congress halts slave importation _____

Britain abolishes the slave trade _____

France outlaws slavery _____

Essay: Read each of the following questions, take some time to organize your thoughts, then compose thorough, meaningful answers for each.

1. Why did slavery become inextricably linked to cotton in the southern mind-set?

2. Why did most southern planters reject industrialization of the region?

3. List and discuss the major differences between the Upper South and Lower South.

4. Describe the life of southern slaves in terms of: work and living conditions, family life, etc.

5. In what ways did slaves retain their human dignity and express resistance?

6. Why were southern slaves apt to embrace the evangelical Christianity of Baptists and Methodists?

7. Describe the life of non-slaveholding southern whites.

8. What were "black codes," and how were these regulations applied to both slaves and free blacks?

9. List and discuss—and offer rebuttals to—the major pro-slavery arguments employed by southerners.

Matching: Match each description or characteristic in the left column with the group most likely to reflect it.

1. ____ Contained leading manufacturing cities.

2. ____ About 25% of southern whites.

3. ____ Worked their own land with family labor.

4. ____ Most prestigious social class.

5. ____ About 15% of southern whites.

6. ____ Led the nation in per capita income.

7. ____ Tended to live in foothills and mountains.

8. ____ Less than 5% of southern white families.

9. ____ 90% of southern slave owners.

10. ____ Owned at least 20 slaves.

11. ____ Slavery on the decline.

12. ____ Agricultural diversification.

13. ____ Tended to be Whigs.

14. ____ Tended to be Democrats.

15. ____ Stood a 50/50 chance of dropping out of the slave-holding class.

16. ____ Lived in remote areas.

17. ____ Most limited to menial, low-paying jobs in cities.

18. ____ Most owned between one and five slaves.

19. ____ Able to use the "gang system."

20. ____ Most likely to live in fear.

A. Planters

B. Small Slaveholders

C. All Slaveholders

D. Yeoman Farmers

E. "Poor Whites"

F. Free Blacks

G. Slaves

H. Upper South

I. Lower South

Map Identification: In the map below, locate each of these items:

7 states of the Lower South
4 border states of the Upper South
4 "middle zone" southern states

Baltimore	Richmond	Atlanta
St. Louis	Nashville	Mobile
Memphis	New Orleans	

MULTIPLE CHOICE ANSWERS:

1. E	11. E
2. E	12. D
3. A	13. E
4. A	14. E
5. E	15. D
6. D.	16. B
7. A	17. E
8. B	18. E
9. C	19. B
10. E	20. C

Chronological Arrangement Answers:

First slaves arrive at Jamestown

Eli Whitney patents the cotton gin

Britain abolishes the slave trade

Congress halts slave importation

Denmark Vessey's Conspiracy

Florida and Texas admitted to the Union

France outlaws slavery

Hinton Helper's *Impending Crisis*

Matching Answers:

1. H
2. C
3. D
4. A
5. E
6. A
7. D (or E)
8. A
9. B
10. A
11. H
12. H
13. A
14. D (or E)
15. B
16. E
17. F
18. B
19. A
20. G

12
The Market Revolution and Social Reform

KEY TOPICS

✓ **The Transportation and Industrial Revolutions**
✓ **Reform Movements**

CHAPTER OUTLINE

I. Industrial Change and Urbanization
    A. The Transportation Revolution
        1. Steamboats and canals
        2. Railroads
        3. Government and the transportation revolution
    B. Cities and Immigrants
        1. The port cities
        2. Inland cities
        3. New industrial cities
        4. Immigration
    C. The Industrial Revolution
        1. Sources of labor
        2. Technological gains
    D. Growing Inequality and New Classes
        1. The new middle class
        2. Women and the cult of domesticity
        3. The working classes
        4. Early trade unions

II. Reform and Moral Order
    A. The Benevolent Empire
    B. The Temperance Movement
    C. Women's Role in Reform
    D. Backlash Against Benevolence

III. Institutions and Social Improvement
    A. School Reform
    B. Prisons, Workhouses, and Asylums
        1. Workhouses
        2. Asylums for the mentally ill
    C. Utopian Alternatives
        1. A distinctly national literature

IV. Abolitionism and Women's Rights
    A. Rejecting Colonization
    B. Abolitionism

C. The Women's Rights Movement
D. Political Antislavery

V. Conclusion

SELF-TESTING

Multiple Choice: In the blanks below, write the letter of the BEST response.

1. _____ For a Philadelphia manufacturer in 1815, it was easier and cheaper to
   a. ship your products across the Atlantic Ocean to Europe than to the interior areas of the States.
   b. transport your products across the state to Pittsburgh than to ship them to England.

2. _____ The Erie Canal connected
   a. Albany and New York City.
   b. Albany and Buffalo.
   c. Baltimore and Philadelphia.
   d. Pittsburgh and Cleveland.
   e. Cincinnati and Cleveland.

3. _____ Most antebellum railroad trunk lines connected
   a. the North and South.
   b. the industrial centers of the Northeast.
   c. Omaha and San Francisco.
   d. the old Northeast and the old Northwest.

4. _____ The supremacy of the federal government to regulate interstate commerce was affirmed in the case of
   a. *McCulloch v. Maryland.*
   b. *Gibbons v. Ogden.*
   c. *Fletcher v. Peck.*
   d. *Charles River Bridge v. Warren Bridge.*

5. _____ Most immigrants in the first half of the nineteenth century arrived from
   a. Germany.
   b. Ireland.
   c. Asia.
   d. All of these answers are correct.
   e. Only a and b are correct.

6. _____ The system whereby local merchants furnished raw materials to rural households, and paid them a piece rate to convert them into manufactured products, was known as the _____ system.
   a. Waltham
   b. putting-out
   c. Rhode Island
   d. American
   e. Lowell

7. _____ Workers who were honing the skills of a particular craft but who still needed to save enough capital to start their own businesses were called
   a. lazy and shiftless.
   b. apprentices.
   c. journeymen.
   d. migrants.
   e. semi-skilled.

8. _____ The American system of manufacturing
   a. transformed the technology of machine tool production.
   b. involved low-cost, standardized mass production.
   c. involved interchangeable parts stamped out by machines.
   d. was characterized by all of these.
   e. Only b and c are correct.

9. _____ In the first half of the nineteenth century, living standards for most Americans
   a. improved, as per capita income doubled.
   b. remained about the same as the eighteenth century.
   c. declined, as class distinctions widened.
   d. declined sharply as the result of the new flood of immigration.

10. _____ The "new middle class" was composed of
   a. nonmanual workers.
   b. office and store clerks.
   c. sales agents and independent retailers.
   d. those in managerial positions.
   e. all of these Americans.

11. _____ During the Industrial Revolution in the United States, the role of most women was all of the following EXCEPT
   a. serving as the spiritual head of the household.
   b. idealized and romanticized.
   c. to bear large numbers of children for her husband.
   d. to refrain from the competitive, morally corrupt worlds of business and politics.

12. _____ The first national labor union was the
   a. Knights of Labor.
   b. American Federation of Labor.
   c. Teamsters.
   d. National Trades Union.
   e. Congress of Industrial Organizations.

13. _____ In the mid-nineteenth century, Americans joined "nativist" organizations because
   a. they had heard rumors of another pan-Indian plan to take back North America.
   b. they sought to curb mass immigration.
   c. they wanted to limit the political impact and rights of Catholic immigrants.
   d. of all of these goals.
   e. Only b and c are correct.

14. _____ In general, the Sabbatarian movement was successful in getting businesses and government agencies to close on Sundays.
    a. True
    b. False

15. _____ The temperance movement
    a. had a greater impact on more Americans than any other reform effort.
    b. rested on the belief that persuasion was more influential than coercion.
    c. rested on the belief that individuals had to decide to free themselves from sin.
    d. believed that alcohol was responsible for crime, poverty, and broken families.
    e. did all of these.

16. _____ The Church of Jesus Christ of Latter-day Saints
    a. represented a backlash against the "benevolent empire" of middle-class evangelical reformers.
    b. concurred with and participated fully in most reform movements.
    c. defined communal beliefs based on shared gender roles.
    d. required giving a "tithe" of 20 percent of one's income.

17. _____ Horace Mann's proposals for mandatory public schools were opposed most by the
    a. Whig Party.
    b. Democratic Party.
    c. Liberty Party.
    d. Know-Nothing Party.

18. _____ The Shakers were known for all of the following EXCEPT
    a. widespread appeal and a large following.
    b. gender equality.
    c. enforced sexual denial.
    d. ecstatic, ritualized dancing.
    e. exquisite craft work such as furniture.

19. _____ "Transcendentalism" relied upon _____ to grasp reality
    a. divine revelation
    b. intuition and emotion
    c. sensory input
    d. reason and inquiry

20. _____ One of the earliest "solutions" to the slavery issue suggested
    a. immediate emancipation.
    b. gradual emancipation.
    c. African colonization.
    d. voluntary manumission.

21. _____ Abolitionists, relying upon reason to propel their argument, tended to avoid the emotionalism associated with evangelical revivalists.
    a. True
    b. False

22. _____ In mid-nineteenth century America, "Slave Power" came to suggest all of the following EXCEPT
   a. the dominance of American politics by the southern planter class.
   b. a conspiracy on the part of southern planters to spread slavery into the West.
   c. that the loss of white liberties—rather than black bondage—was the most serious threat associated with slavery.
   d. the threat of a mass, armed uprising by legions of black slaves.

Chronological Arrangement: Rearrange the list of events below by **rewriting** each item in correct chronological sequence into the blanks provided.

Mormons move to Utah _____

Texas admitted to the Union _____

Panic of 1837 _____

Britain emancipates slaves _____

Garrison publishes the *Liberator* _____

Seneca Falls Convention _____

Slater builds first cotton factory in America _____

Eli Whitney patents the Cotton Gin _____

Brook Farm established _____

Fulton demonstrates his steamboat _____

Essay: Read each of the following questions, take some time to organize your thoughts, then compose thorough, meaningful answers for each.

1. Describe the impact of the transportation revolution upon nineteenth-century America.

2. Describe the incremental changes in domestic manufacturing between 1800 and 1850.

3. In what ways were the traditional roles of women changed by the Industrial Revolution?

4. What was the "benevolent empire"? What did reformers want to happen?

5. Discuss the origins of the Utopian movement. Why did most communal experiments ultimately fail?

6. Why was abolitionism originally associated with women's rights? Why did the two movements split?

7. What was the goal of the Seneca Falls Convention in 1848? What were the results?

8. In what important ways did the "Slave Power" notion change the abolitionist crusade?

9. What impact did Britain's emancipation of slaves have upon emancipation movements elsewhere?

Matching: Match each description in the left column with the person it most likely describes. (Beware: Not all names will be used!)

1. _____ Began the steamboat building boom when he sent his *Clermont* 150 miles up the Hudson

2. _____ English mechanic whose memory enabled him to construct a water-powered spinning mill

3. _____ New England preacher whose drive to restore morality included remembering the Sabbath.

4. _____ Impressionable young New Yorker; his personal revelations became the *Book of Mormon*

5. _____ Former Whig politician who became the tireless champion of compulsory public education

6. _____ Horrified by the inhuman treatment of the mentally ill, she led the movement to improve asylums

7. _____ Escaped slave who became a spellbinding lecturer and founder of the abolitionist *North Star*

8. _____ His Oneida Community featured plural marriage, community nurseries, and common property

9. _____ Former Unitarian minister who taught that truth could be found by transcending human institutions

10. _____ Lived for 16 months in isolation at Walden Pond in a quest for self-discovery.

11. _____ Massachusetts printer whose passion for abolition became fused with women's rights

12. _____ One of two planter-born sisters, she became a powerful public lecturer on abolition

13. _____ President who wanted to colonize ex-slaves in Africa; his name became the capital of Liberia

14. _____ Former president, then congressman who argued *Amistad*; tried to get around Democrats' "gag rule"

A. Angelina Grimké

B. Lyman Beecher

C. Henry Clay

D. Frederick Douglass

E. Ralph Waldo Emerson

F. Robert Fulton

G. William Lloyd Garrison

H. Horace Mann

I. Washington Irving

J. Joseph Smith

K. James K. Polk

L. Dorothea Dix

M. James Monroe

N. John Humphrey Noyes

O. Robert Owen

P. Edgar A. Poe

Q. John Q. Adams

R. Lucretia Mott

S. Samuel Slater

T. Henry David Thoreau

U. Upton Sinclair

V. Eugene Debs

W. Walt Whitman

MULTIPLE CHOICE ANSWERS:

1. A	11. C	21. B
2. B	12. D	22. D
3. D	13. E	
4. B	14. B	
5. E	15. E	
6. B	16. A	
7. C	17. B	
8. D	18. A	
9. A	19. B	
10. E	20. C	

CHRONOLOGICAL ARRANGEMENT ANSWERS:

Slater builds first cotton factory in America

Eli Whitney patents the cotton gin

Fulton demonstrates his steamboat

Garrison publishes the *Liberator*

Britain emancipates slaves

Panic of 1837

Brook Farm established

Texas admitted to the Union

Mormons move to Utah

Seneca Falls Convention

Matching Answers:

1. F
2. S
3. B
4. J
5. H
6. L
7. D
8. N
9. E
10. T
11. G
12. A
13. M
14. Q

13
The Way West

KEY TOPICS

- ✓ **The Spread of Agriculture**
- ✓ **Native Peoples of the West**
- ✓ **White Inroads into the West**
- ✓ **Acquiring Texas, Oregon, and California**

CHAPTER OUTLINE

I.   The Agricultural Frontier
    A.   The Crowded East
    B.   The Old Northwest
        1.   A mosaic of settlements
    C.   The Old Southwest

II.   The Frontier of the Plains Indians
    A.   Tribal Lands
    B.   The Fur Traders
    C.   The Oregon Trail

III.   The Mexican Borderlands
    A.   The Peoples of the Southwest
    B.   The Americanization of Texas
    C.   The Push into California and the Southwest
        1.   California
        2.   New Mexico
        3.   Utah

IV.   Politics, Expansion, and War
    A.   Manifest Destiny
    B.   The Mexican War

V.   Conclusion

SELF-TESTING

Multiple Choice: In the blanks below, write the letter of the BEST response.

1. _____ Just as whites considered their civilization superior to that of Native People, some Indians, likewise, thought white Americans were barbaric.
   a. True.
   b. False.

2. _____ What percentage of Americans lived west of the Appalachians in 1850?
   a. 10%.
   b. 25%.
   c. 50%.
   d. 70%.

3. _____ Contributing to the westward movement of Americans in the first half of the nineteenth century was (were)
   a. the declining fertility of eastern farmland.
   b. subdivisions and concentrations of landholdings.
   c. the availability and affordability of western land.
   d. the American linkage of land-holding with republican virtue.
   e. All of these answers are correct.

4. _____ Migrants from Pennsylvania and New Jersey were likely to settle in
   a. northern Ohio and Indiana.
   b. central Ohio and Indiana.
   c. southern Ohio and Indiana.
   d. Kentucky and Tennessee.

5. _____ The main ingredients of southwest cooking (then and now) include(d)
   a. corn and pork.
   b. wheat and beef.
   c. venison and fish.
   d. chicken and potatoes.

6. _____ The original plan for an Indian colonization zone called for an area from the
   a. Platte River to the Red River.
   b. Missouri Compromise line to the Red River.
   c. Mississippi River to the Indian Meridian.
   d. Mississippi River to the Rocky Mountains.
   e. Red River to the Nueces River.

7. _____ Which most revolutionized life for the Natives of the Plains?
   a. availability of firearms
   b. arrival of Spanish horses
   c. discovery of new buffalo hunting techniques
   d. discovery of new uses for buffalo
   e. trading with white Americans

8. _____ The annual meeting of mountain men, Natives, and traders from the Rocky Mountain Fur Company in a pre-arranged location in the Rockies was called the
a. American system.
b. putting-out system.
c. rendezvous.
d. traders' reunion.

9. _____ The first Americans to venture systematically to Oregon were
a. mountain men.
b. settlers.
c. land speculators.
d. missionaries.
e. hide and tallow traders.

10. _____ During the heyday of the Oregon Trail
a. there were few Indian problems.
b. most migrants died from disease and accidents.
c. most migrants thought of the Plains as a great desert to be crossed.
d. more than six thousand Americans moved to Oregon.
e. all of these characterized the era.

11. _____ Spain divided the peoples of their New World into four groups. Which of these was NOT one of those groups?
a. Indians.
b. *Presidios.*
c. *Mestizos.*
d. *Criollos.*
e. Spaniards.

12. _____ The main reason why the Mexican government offered land to Americans to entice them to immigrate to Texas was to
a. prevent possible French colonization efforts.
b. furnish a buffer between their northern provinces and predatory Comanches.
c. find a way to harvest economic benefit from the sparsely populated region.
d. entice Britain into an alliance that would challenge the Monroe Doctrine.

13. _____ An American who was given a large tract of land in exchange for bringing new settlers to Texas was called a(n):
a. *empresario.*
b. *presidio.*
c. *Tejano.*
d. *mestizo.*
e. *ranchero.*

14. _____ Mexican armies led by Antonio Lopez de Santa Anna slaughtered Texans at
a. the Alamo.
b. Goliad.
c. San Jacinto.
d. All of these are correct.
e. Only a and b are correct.

15. _____ Mexico tried to strengthen its hold on remote and thinly populated California by
    a. secularizing the mission holdings of the Catholic Church.
    b. privatizing the California economy.
    c. opening trade doors to American businessmen.
    d. all of these methods.

16. _____ Which of the following was the most thinly populated Mexican region in 1840?
    a. Texas.
    b. California.
    c. New Mexico.
    d. Utah.

17. _____ The Mormons were successful in Utah because of
    a. close-knit communities.
    b. the righteous zeal of their members.
    c. concentrating their farms along the slopes of the Wasatch range.
    d. careful organization and planning.
    e. all of these factors.

18. _____ "Manifest Destiny" was most often proclaimed by the _____ Party
    a. Whig
    b. Democratic
    c. Liberty
    d. Know-Nothing

19. _____ The concept of "Manifest Destiny"
    a. derived from the Puritan notion that God ordained them to establish a New Israel.
    b. identified white Americans as the foremost human race.
    c. assumed that expansion would be peaceful.
    d. lumped Indians and Mexicans together as inferior people.
    e. contained all of these notions.

20. _____ President Polk triggered war with Mexico in 1846 by
    a. claiming that American honor had been violated by the refusal of the Mexican government to receive the Slidell delegation.
    b. claiming that American honor had been violated by the Mexican refusal to sell California.
    c. claiming the disputed territory between the Nueces River and the Rio Grande.
    d. placing an American army where the Mexicans would regard it as an invasion.
    e. All of these things incited the war with Mexico.

21. _____ In 1859, in the Rio Grande valley, a revolt occurred because Mexican Americans were angry over violated treaties and racial discrimination by "Anglos."
    a. True.
    b. False.

22. _____ When Manifest Destiny subsided by the end of the 1840s, the United States never again tried to assert its influence in world affairs.
    a. True.
    b. False.

Chronological Arrangement: Rearrange the list of events below by **rewriting** each item in correct chronological sequence into the blanks provided.

Texas wins independence from Mexico _____

(First) Treaty of Ft. Laramie _____

Treaty of Guadalupe Hidalgo _____

Congress creates Indian Territory _____

United States annexes Texas _____

First Rocky Mountain rendezvous _____

Mormons begin Utah settlement _____

Large parties begin the Oregon Trail _____

Mexican War begins _____

Mexico gains its independence from Spain_____

Essay: Read each of the following questions, take some time to organize your thoughts, then compose thorough, meaningful answers for each.

1. What did George Catlin learn from his interview with the Sioux (Lakota) Chief?

2. What was the rendezvous system, who was involved, and what products were involved in the system?

3. Describe life on the Oregon Trail in the mid-1840s.

5. What decisions were made by the Mexican government that led eventually to their loss of both Texas and California?

6. Why did the Latter Day Saints migrate from New York all the way to Utah?

7. How did the concept of Manifest Destiny justify westward expansion in the 1840s?

8. How did the Unites States become involved in a war with Mexico in 1846?

9. How did Manifest Destiny in the 1840s tie together America's philosophical past with future foreign policy?

10. Discuss the conditions in the east that led to the migration westward.

Matching: Match each description in the left column with the person it most likely describes. (Beware: Not all names will be used!)

1. ____ One of the few Americans to value native culture; tried to capture it on canvas before it vanished.

2. ____ General who captured Vera Cruz, and then marched inland to capture Mexico City in September 1847.

3. ____ General whose troops were placed deep in disputed territory to provoke Mexico to war.

4. ____ First American *empresario* and founder of the first American colony in Texas.

5. ____ Flamboyant president of Mexico; he led forces against Texans, then Americans later.

6. ____ Commanded the Texan army; he led Texans to independence at San Jacinto.

7. ____ Following the founder's death, he led Mormons to their final destination in Utah.

8. ____ Expansionist president; compromised with Britain for Oregon; fought Mexico for California.

9. ____ Democratic editor who said it was our "Manifest Destiny to overspread . . . the continent."

A. Stephen Austin

B. Thomas Hart Benton

C. George Catlin

D. Zachary Taylor

E. John Eaton

F. Robert Fulton

G. James Gadsden

H. Sam Houston

I. Winfield Scott

J. Juan Cortina

K. James K. Polk

L. Jason Lee

M. Brigham Young

N. Santa Anna

O. John O'Sullivan

Map Identification: In the map below, locate each of these items:

Indian Territory	Route of Lewis and Clark	Oregon Trail
South Pass	Rendezvous locations	Nueces River
Rio Grande	Santa Fe	Oregon Territory after 1846

MULTIPLE CHOICE ANSWERS:

1. A	11. B	21. A
2. C	12. B	22. B
3. E	13. A	
4. B	14. E	
5. A	15. D	
6. A	16. D	
7. B	17. C	
8. C	18. B	
9. D	19. E	
10. E	20. E	

CHRONOLOGICAL ARRANGEMENT ANSWERS:

Mexico wins independence from Spain

First Rocky Mountain rendezvous

Congress creates Indian Territory

Texas wins independence from Mexico

Large parties begin the Oregon Trail

United States annexes Texas

Mexican War begins

Mormons begin Utah settlement

Treaty of Guadalupe Hidalgo

(First) Treaty of Ft. Laramie

MATCHING ANSWERS:

1. C
2. I
3. D
4. A
5. N
6. H
7. M
8. K
9. O

14

The Politics of Sectionalism

1846–1861

KEY TOPICS

- ✓ **Slavery and the Western Territories**
- ✓ **Political Realignment**
- ✓ **The Perilous Decade of the 1850s**

CHAPTER OUTLINE

I. Slavery in the Territories
    A. The Wilmot Proviso
    B. The Election of 1848
    C. The Gold Rush
    D. The Compromise of 1850
    E. Response to the Fugitive Slave Act
    F. *Uncle Tom's Cabin*
    G. The Election of 1852

II. Political Realignment
    A. Young America's Foreign Misadventures
    B. Stephen Douglas's Railroad Proposal
    C. The Kansas-Nebraska Act
    D. "Bleeding Kansas"
    E. Know-Nothings and Republicans: Religion and Politics
    F. The Election of 1856
    G. The Dred Scott Case
    H. The Lecompton Constitution
    I. The Religious Revival of 1857–1858
    J. The Lincoln-Douglas Debates

III. The Road to Disunion
    A. North-South Differences
        1. Economic differences
        2. Social and religious differences
        3. The effects of slavery
    B. John Brown's Raid
    C. The Election of 1860
    D. Secession Begins
    E. Presidential Inaction
    F. Peace Proposals
    G. Lincoln's Views on Secession
    H. Fort Sumter: The Tug Comes

IV. Conclusion

SELF-TESTING

Multiple Choice: In the blanks below, write the letter of the **best** response.

1. _____ Which of the following was NOT one of the proposed solutions to the problem of slavery in the territories?
   a. excluding slavery from the territories altogether
   b. partitioning the West by extending the Missouri Compromise line to the Pacific
   c. postponing expansion by creating settlement-free zones
   d. allowing a territory's residents to decide the issue for themselves
   e. allowing slaveowners to take their property into any territory they desired

2. _____ Which of the following issues central to westward expansion was NOT clouded by the slavery debate?
   a. the admission of Texas
   b. the Mexican War
   c. the admission of California
   d. the first transcontinental railroad
   e. All of these were entangled with the slavery issue.

3. _____ Which of the following institutions was affected by the slavery issue?
   a. Whig Party
   b. Democratic Party
   c. Baptist Church
   d. Methodist Church
   e. All of these were affected.

4. _____ The concept of allowing the residents of a prospective new state to decide their own free/slave status was called:
   a. risky and foolish.
   b. popular sovereignty.
   c. populism.
   d. the American System.

5. _____ The Free-Soil Party was composed of those Americans who
   a. wanted an immediate end of slavery.
   b. wanted to keep the West free from the competition of slave labor.
   c. were Southern Whigs.
   d. wanted all of these.

6. _____ Those who profited the most from the California Gold Rush were
   a. the first to get there, removing surface gold with techniques such as panning.
   b. those who supplied the hopeful miners.
   c. large companies that could afford heavy machinery.
   d. Indian tribes who owned most of California's mineral rights.
   e. Both b and c are correct.

7. _____ Henry Clay proposed to solve the problem of California's admission as a state by
   a. admitting California as a free state.
   b. granting popular sovereignty to New Mexico and Utah.
   c. ending the slave trade in Washington, D.C.
   d. giving the South the fugitive slave law they had been demanding.
   e. all of these measures.

8. _____ The Fugitive Slave Law
   a. enabled white southerners to pursue runaway slaves into northern states.
   b. made re-enslavement a real possibility for runaways.
   c. led to the capture and enslavement of northern blacks who had never been slaves.
   d. caused many African-Americans to flee further north to Canada.
   e. did all of these things.

9. _____ *Uncle Tom's Cabin* had widespread northern appeal because
   a. Stowe evoked many strong emotions.
   b. Stowe's characters seem real rather than abstract.
   c. Stowe's themes reached Americans in the midst of a religious revival.
   d. Stowe suggested that slavery was a sin and subverted Christianity.
   e. of all of these reasons.

10. _____ In the presidential election of 1852, the _____ Party suffered schisms from which it would never recover.
   a. Whig
   b. Democratic
   c. Free-Soil
   d. Republican
   e. Libertarian

11. _____ The Ostend Manifesto was an embarrassing American attempt to grab
   a. Cuba.
   b. Nicaragua.
   c. Panama.
   d. Baja California.

12. _____ Stephen Douglas's desire to extend a railroad from Chicago to the Pacific was problematic, in that
   a. the route would cross a portion of Indian Territory.
   b. southerners didn't want a transcontinental railroad with a northern terminus.
   c. the proposed route lay north of the Missouri Compromise line and thus would give the North one or more new states.
   d. All of these are correct.

13. _____ Kansas Territory was more likely than Nebraska Territory to become a slave state because of all of the following EXCEPT
   a. its more fertile soil.
   b. Native Americans assigned to the Kansas portion of Indian Territory wanted to adopt a slave system for themselves.
   c. its more southerly—and hence more favorable—climate.
   d. it was adjacent to Missouri, a slave state already.

14. _____ The Kansas-Nebraska Act led to
   a. a race to populate Kansas with pro-slavery and abolitionist partisans.
   b. a sporadic, violent civil war.
   c. fraudulent voting to select a constitutional convention.
   d. a legal but fraudulent government and an extra-legal but popular government.
   e. All of these answers are correct.

15. _____ Know-Nothings were those who opposed
   a. slavery.
   b. immigration.
   c. westward expansion.
   d. education.
   e. alcoholic beverages.

16. _____ The Free-Soil Party attracted
   a. Conscience Whigs.
   b. disaffected northern Democrats.
   c. former Liberty Party members.
   d. all of these voters.

17. _____ In the case of *Dred Scott v. Sanford*, Chief Justice Roger Taney
   a. stated that blacks were not citizens and, therefore, could not sue.
   b. stated that Scott's temporary residence in free states did not make him free.
   c. reflected his view that the Missouri Compromise was unconstitutional.
   d. implied that slavery could exist anywhere, even in all northern states.
   e. did all of these.

18. _____ The religious revivals of the late 1850s urged converts and followers to keep their spiritual lives separate from their politics.
   a. True
   b. False

19. _____ Abraham Lincoln debated Stephen Douglas in their race for
   a. the presidency.
   b. Douglas's U.S. Senate seat.
   c. Lincoln's U.S. House seat.
   d. the governorship of Illinois.

20. _____ Abraham Lincoln
   a. was at first ambivalent on slavery but later became an abolitionist.
   b. was consistent both in his opposition to slavery as well as his attitudes concerning race relations.
   c. was firm in his opposition to slavery, but his ambiguity toward race relations evolved.
   d. was elusive—hesitant to reveal his attitudes toward issues of race.

21. _____ John Brown's raid on the arsenal in Harpers Ferry
   a. made him a martyr in the North.
   b. increased southerners' fears of a general, armed slave uprising.
   c. suggested to southerners an attack not from within but from an external enemy.
   d. did all of these.

22. ____ Which of the following was NOT a candidate for president in 1860?
   a. Stephen A. Douglas
   b. John C. Breckinridge
   c. Abraham Lincoln
   d. John C. Frémont

23. ____ When confronted with the Ft. Sumter issue, President Lincoln chose to
   a. assert the idea of Federal Union by using the navy to defend the fort.
   b. allow southern tempers to cool by releasing the fort to Charleston.
   c. ordered an immediate evacuation of the fort.
   d. to diffuse southern anger by re-provisioning the fort with unarmed ships.
   e. do all of these things.

Chronological Arrangement: Rearrange the list of events below by **rewriting** each item in correct chronological sequence into the blanks provided.

Compromise of 1850   _____

Abraham Lincoln elected   _____

Preston Brooks canes Charles Sumner   _____

Gold discovered in California   _____

Lincoln-Douglas debates   _____

Kansas-Nebraska Act   _____

Dred Scott v. Sanford   _____

John Brown raids Harpers Ferry   _____

Mexican War and the Wilmot Proviso   _____

Uncle Tom's Cabin published   _____

Essay: Read each of the following questions, take some time to organize your thoughts, then compose thorough, meaningful answers for each.

1. List and discuss the major reasons why northerners were unwilling to allow the extension of slavery into the new western territories.

2. Explain the series of proposals known as the Compromise of 1850. Describe the method of its passage.

3. Describe the various reactions to *Uncle Tom's Cabin*: by northern whites, by southern whites.

4. Why did the Kansas-Nebraska Act stir such turmoil, even among southerners who stood to gain potential new slave states?

5. Discuss the evolving political landscape of the 1850s. Why did some parties succeed and others fail?

6. Discuss the *Dred Scott* case. Why were northerners so incensed by Taney's opinions?

7. What was the problem—in Kansas and outside—with the Lecompton Constitution?

8. List and discuss some of the results of the religious revivals of the late 1850s.

9. What did John Brown feel called to accomplish? How did he create trouble in **two** places?

10. How did the circumstances in the presidential campaign of 1860 result in the election of the candidate of a purely sectional party?

11. Why did the states of the Lower South secede first? Why were they then joined by the states of the middle South?

Matching: Match each description or characteristic in the left column with the group most likely to reflect it.

1. _____ "Hamiltonian"(industrial, more urban)   A. North

2. _____ "Jeffersonian" (agricultural, rural)   B. South

3. _____ Ingrained martial tradition   C. Both Sections

4. _____ Witnessed political party splits   D. Neither Section

5. _____ Fifteen percent of nation's factories

6. _____ Six percent illiteracy rate

7. _____ Large, ethnically diverse white population

8. _____ Biracial with 35 percent African American

9. _____ Stagnant growth, neither relied heavily on agriculture or industy

10. _____ About 20,000 miles of track, effectively linking east and west

Matching: Match each description in the left column with the person it most likely describes. (Beware: Not all names will be used. Some will be used **more than once!**)

1. _____ Mexican War general; had never voted but was the   A. Daniel Webster
successful Whig candidate in 1848

B. Harriet B. Stowe

2. _____ Old former president; ran surprisingly strongly as
the Free-Soil candidate in 1848   C. John C. Frémont

3. _____ Won national attention and acclaim through his   D. Stephen Douglas
Senate campaign in 1858

E. Edmund Ruffin

4. _____ Proposed compromise provoking historic
Senate debate in 1850   F. Millard Fillmore

5. _____ At personal political peril, this great Massachusetts G. Johann Sutter
orator lent his support to the Compromise of 1850

H. Henry Clay

6. _____ New Yorker; second "accidental" president; his art
of the deal enabled passage of the Compromise   I. Winfield Scott

7. _____ Envisioned an urban, industrial West, linked to the   J. John Brown
East by a vast railroad network

K. James K. Polk

8. ____ Escaped slave whose National Black Convention resolved that *Uncle Tom's Cabin* was "a work…by the finger of God"

9. ____ Abolitionist novelist; raised in a family of Protestant ministers and evangelicals

10. ____ Mexican War general, who in the election of 1852 was the last serious Whig candidate for president

11. ____ New Hampshire moderate; as president, increasingly deferred to southerners on slavery

12. ____ Popular military hero; became the very first Republican candidate for president in 1856

13. ____ His railroad schemes led to abrogation of Indian treaties and to "Bleeding Kansas"

14. ____ Considered a "rustic celebrity" by New England abolitionists, his followers killed in Kansas

L. Abraham Lincoln

M. John Marshall

N. John Humphrey Noyes

O. Osceola

P. Franklin Pierce

Q. James Buchanan

R. Benjamin Rush

S. Frederick Douglass

T. Henry D. Thoreau

U. Charles Sumner

V. Martin Van Buren

W. William Walker

X. Preston Brooks

Y. William Yancey

Z. Zachary Taylor

MULTIPLE CHOICE ANSWERS

1. C	11. A	21. D
2. E	12. D	22. D
3. E	13. B	23. D
4. B	14. E	
5. B	15. B	
6. E	16. D	
7. E	17. E	
8. E	18. B	
9. E	19. B	
10. A	20. C	

CHRONOLOGICAL ARRANGEMENT ANSWERS:

Mexican War and the Wilmot Proviso

Gold discovered in California

Compromise of 1850

Uncle Tom's Cabin published

Kansas/Nebraska Act

Preston Brooks canes Charles Sumner

Dred Scott v. Sanford

Lincoln/Douglas debates

John Brown raids Harper's Ferry

Abraham Lincoln elected

MATCHING ANSWERS:

1. A
2. B
3. B
4. C
5. B
6. A
7. A
8. B
9. D
10. A

MATCHING ANSWERS:

1. Z	7. D	13. D
2. V	8. S	14. J
3. G	9. B	
4. H	10. I	
5. A	11. P	
6. F	12. C	

15
The Civil War

KEY TOPICS

- ✓ **North and South: A Balance Sheet**
- ✓ **The War's Stages and Turning Points**
- ✓ **The Transforming Impact of the Civil War**

CHAPTER OUTLINE

I. Mobilization, North and South
    A. War Fever
    B. The North's Advantage in Resources
    C. Leaders, Governments, and Strategies
        1. Jefferson Davis and the South
        2. Abraham Lincoln and the North
        3. Lincoln's fight for the border states
        4. Strategies and tactics

II. The Early War, 1861–1862
    A. First Bull Run
    B. The War in the West
    C. Reassessing the War: The Human Toll
    D. The War in the East

III. Turning Points, 1862–1863
    A. The Naval War and the Diplomatic War
        1. The naval war
        2. The diplomatic front
    B. Antietam
    C. Emancipation
        1. The Emancipation Proclamation
        2. "Stealing" freedom
        3. Black troops in the Union Army
    D. From Fredericksburg to Gettysburg
        1. Fredericksburg
        2. Chancellorsville
        3. Gettysburg
    E. Vicksburg, Chattanooga, and the West
        1. Vicksburg
        2. Chattanooga
        3. The war in the Trans-Mississippi West

IV. War Transforms the North
    A. Wartime Legislation and Politics
        1. Suppressing dissent

2.   Creating a national economy
3.   Conscription and the draft riots
- B.   The Northern Economy
  1.   Trade unions and strikebreakers
  2.   Profiteers and corruption
- C.   Northern Women and the War

V.   The Confederacy Disintegrates
- A.   Southern Politics
- B.   Southern Faith
- C.   The Southern Economy
- D.   Southern Women and the War

VI.   The Union Prevails, 1864–1865
- A.   Grant's Plan to End the War
  1.   From the Wilderness to Cold Harbor
  2.   Atlanta
- B.   The Election of 1864 and Sherman's March
  1.   The Republican victory
  2.   Sherman's march to the sea
  3.   Lincoln's second inaugural
  4.   Arming the Confederacy's slaves
- C.   The Road to Appomattox and the Death of Lincoln
  1.   The surrender at Appomattox
  2.   The death of Lincoln

VII.   Conclusion

SELF-TESTING

Multiple Choice: In the blanks below, write the letter of the **best** response.

1. _____ At the beginning of the Civil War, both major political parties in the North united behind Lincoln and the war effort.
   a. True
   b. False

2. _____ At the onset of the Civil War, which was NOT a typical reason why most recruits on both sides signed up to fight?
   a. Patriotism
   b. To defend their homes
   c. High pay scales
   d. Glory and adventure

3. _____ Which side, to finance the war, issued "greenbacks" and instituted the nation's first income tax?
   a. North
   b. South

4. ____ Which side, to raise troop strength, instituted the nation's first draft of its citizens?
    a. North
    b. South

5. ____ Which of the following was NOT one of the precarious, slave "border" states?
    a. Missouri
    b. Kentucky
    c. Kansas
    d. Maryland
    e. Delaware

6. ____ The overall strategy of the Confederacy included all of the following EXCEPT:
    a. required fighting only a defensive battle.
    b. relied on waiting until the North lost its will to continue.
    c. relied on the conscription of slaves fight in the Confederate army.
    d. relied on having sufficient resources to outlast northern resolve.
    e. demanded patience.

7. ____ The overall strategy of the North involved all of the following EXCEPT:
    a. an alliance with Britain wherein they would only sell arms to the North.
    b. detaching the trans-Appalachian West from the rest of the South.
    c. holding Missouri, Kentucky, and Tennessee.
    d. capturing the Confederate capital at Richmond.
    e. controlling the Mississippi River.

8. ____ Because Manassas Junction was so close to Washington, D.C., many from the city dressed in their finery and drove out with their picnic lunches to watch the battle.
    a. True
    b. False

9. ____ In the early stage of the war, Grant's troops in the west won an important victory at
    a. Fort Henry.
    b. Fort Donelson.
    c. Shiloh.
    d. All of these places were sites of important Union victories.

10. ____ Casualty rates were inordinately high in the Civil War because
    a. generals were experimenting with revolutionary new methods.
    b. generals were taking unnecessary risks to achieve victory.
    c. military technology had progressed but battlefield tactics had not.
    d. soldiers wanted to "go down in a blaze of glory."

11. ____ The biggest killer of soldiers during the war was
    a. wounds from rifles.
    b. wounds from exploding artillery shells.
    c. disease.
    d. primitive medical procedures.

12. _____ Before he could make any significant move toward emancipation, Lincoln needed

    a. Congressional approval.
    b. to be reelected.
    c. a significant military victory.
    d. diplomatic assurances from Britain and France.

13. _____ Confederate use of cotton as a bargaining chip succeeded in winning diplomatic recognition from

    a. Britain.
    b. France.
    c. Spain.
    d. Austria.
    e. None of these.

14. _____ Which of the following groups objected most to the idea of emancipation?

    a. The Union army
    b. The Republican Congress
    c. Irish Catholic immigrants
    d. Northern citizens

15. _____ During the war, the term "contraband" came to mean

    a. incoming goods intercepted by Union naval vessels.
    b. prisoners of war.
    c. runaway and freed slaves.
    d. valuables taken from southern homes by Sherman's army.

16. _____ The number of captives who died in Union and Confederate prisons was about

    a. 5,000.
    b. 10,000.
    c. 25,000.
    d. 56,000.

17. _____ The great and bloody battle of Gettysburg began as a Confederate attempt to get at the town's supply of

    a. weapons.
    b. food.
    c. medical supplies.
    d. prostitutes.
    e. shoes.

18. _____ Using executive authority to suppress dissent, president Lincoln

    a. authorized the execution of hundreds of dissidents.
    b. suspended the writ of habeas corpus.
    c. arrested and imprisoned newspaper editors who published negative stories.
    d. tried to rig off-year elections to maintain Republican control of Congress.
    e. tried to "pack" the Supreme Court with justices favorable to his programs.

19. ____ In 1863, riots occurred in New York because of
    a. racial antagonism.
    b. social class antagonism.
    c. anti-draft anger.
    d. all of these problems.

20. ____ During the war, the northern economy
    a. experienced severe panic.
    b. dipped briefly, then boomed.
    c. brought prosperity only to a few profiteers.
    d. shut women out of the workforce.

21. ____ A fundamental problem that affected the Confederacy's ultimate success was their unflagging attachment to states' rights.
    a. True
    b. False

22. ____ In the waning stages of the war, that which was desired most by blacks who were still enslaved on southern plantations was:
    a. revenge.
    b. education.
    c. Christianity.
    d. freedom.

23. ____ Northern Democrats who opposed the war and would have settled for peace without emancipation were known as
    a. jerks.
    b. cowards.
    c. traitors.
    d. Copperheads.

24. ____ That which outlawed slavery was the
    a. Emancipation Proclamation.
    b. Gettysburg Address.
    c. Thirteenth Amendment.
    d. Fourteenth Amendment.

Chronological Arrangement: Rearrange the list of events below by **rewriting** each item in correct chronological sequence into the blanks provided.

Lee surrenders to Grant   _____

Abraham Lincoln first elected   _____

Sherman captures Atlanta   _____

McClellan loses Peninsula Campaign   _____

Battle of Gettysburg   _____

Confederates fire on Ft. Sumter   _____

McClellan forfeits Antietam opportunity   _____

Lincoln assassinated   _____

First Bull Run (Manassas)   _____

Emancipation Proclamation applied   _____

Essay: Read each of the following questions, take some time to organize your thoughts, then compose thorough, meaningful answers for each.

1. Most southern whites did NOT own slaves. Why, then, did they fight eagerly in the Civil War?

2. Compare the war strategies of the North and South.

3. Describe the life of the average foot soldier in the Civil War.

4. George B. McClellan was well-liked by the Army of the Potomac. Why, then, did Lincoln have to fire him—**twice**?

5. For what reasons was England interested in the American Civil War? What kept Britain out?

6. How and why did Lincoln carefully word the Emancipation Proclamation?

7. In what ways was the northern economy affected by the war?

8. How did the war affect gender roles, both in the North and South?

9. Why did the North win (or the South lose)?

10. Referring to Lincoln's comments, what broader meaning(s) did he attach to the Civil War?

Matching: Match each description, characteristic, or pre-war advantage in the left column with the section of the country most likely to reflect it.

1. _____ Largely volunteer, citizen armies

2. _____ Superior military leadership

3. _____ Needed to conquer the other to win

4. _____ Needed to fight only a defensive war

5. _____ Believed the war would be short

6. _____ Naval advantage

7. _____ Diversified economy

8. _____ Hoped for help from abroad

9. _____ Larger population

10. _____ Believed that God was on their side

11. _____ Inability to unite together as a nation

12. _____ Armies and materials were stretched too thin

13. _____ Railroad system twice the size of the other side's

14. _____ President lacked people and political skills

15. _____ President generated affection with folksy humor

A. North

B. South

C. Both Sections

D. Neither Section

Matching: Match each Civil War battle in the left column with the outcome from the right column.

1. _____ First Bull Run (Manassas)

2. _____ Shiloh

3. _____ Antietam

4. _____ Fredericksburg

5. _____ Chancellorsville

6. _____ Gettysburg

7. _____ Vicksburg

8. _____ Wilderness

9. _____ Atlanta

10. _____ Petersburg

A. Union victory

B. Confederate victory

C. Indecisive

Matching: Match each description in the left column with the person it most likely describes. (Beware: Not all names will be used. Some will be used **more than once!**)

1. _____ President of the Confederacy

2. _____ First Republican president

3. _____ Reprimanded a Confederate general for not shooting; Union officer; killed accidentally at Chancellorsville

4. _____ "Little Mac;" he was within sight of Richmond when he lost his nerve, and abandoned the Peninsula

5. _____ Confederate general with a reserved and aristocratic bearing; not afraid to take risks

6. _____ Southern-sympathizing actor; led the conspiracy to kill Lincoln and others

7. _____ Though he had Lee's battle plans in hand, he waited hours before attacking at Antietam

8. _____ Refused Lincoln's call to command claiming he was incompetent

9. _____ His success at risk-taking perhaps made him over-confident on the third day at Gettysburg

10. _____ Offered dedication of the federal cemetery at Gettysburg

11. _____ His Union forces in the west won at Ft. Henry, Ft. Donelson, Shiloh, and Vicksburg

12. _____ Cherokee Confederate; fought at Battle of Pea Ridge; became a brigadier general

13. _____ Finally in command of northern forces, he applied relentless pressure on Lee's southern forces

14. _____ Captured Atlanta, then cut a swath of destruction to Savannah, then north into the Carolinas

15. _____ Nominated by the Democrats to run against Lincoln in 1864

16. _____ Said that God was punishing the South for slavery, and the North for letting slavery go unchecked

A. Ambrose Burnside

B. George B. McClellan

C. Clara Barton

D. Jefferson Davis

E. Jubal Early

F. David Farragut

G. Gideon Welles

H. Henry W. Halleck

I. Irvin McDowell

J. Thomas J. Jackson

K. Nathan Bedford Forrest

L. Abraham Lincoln

M. George G. Meade

N. Napoleon III

O. John B. Hood

P. John Pope

Q. Victoria

R. Robert E. Lee

S. Stand Watie

T. William T. Sherman

U. Ulysses Grant

V. Clement Vallandigham

W. John Wilkes Booth

X. Maximilian

Map Identification: On the map below, locate each of these battle sites:

Fort Sumter	Bull Run	The Peninsula
Shiloh	Antietam	Gettysburg
Vicksburg	Chattanooga	Atlanta

MULTIPLE CHOICE ANSWERS:

1. A	11. C	21. A
2. C	12. A	22. D
3. A	13. E	23. D
4. B	14. C	24. C
5. C	15. C	
6. C	16. D	
7. A	17. E	
8. A	18. B	
9. D	19. D	
10. C	20. B	

CHRONOLOGICAL ARRANGEMENT ANSWERS:

Abraham Lincoln first elected

Confederates fire on Ft. Sumter

First Bull Run (Manassas)

McClellan loses Peninsula Campaign

McClellan forfeits Antietam opportunity

Emancipation Proclamation applied

Battle of Gettysburg

Sherman captures Atlanta

Lee surrenders to Grant

Lincoln assassinated

MATCHING ANSWERS:

1. C	6. A	11. B
2. B	7. A	12. B
3. A	8. C	13. A
4. B	9. A	14. B
5. C	10. C	15. A

MATCHING ANSWERS:

1. B	5. B	9. A
2. A	6. A	10. A
3. A	7. A	
4. B	8. B	

MATCHING ANSWERS:

1. D	7. B	13. U
2. L	8. A	14. T
3. J	9. R	15. B
4. B	10. L	16. L
5. R	11. U	
6. W	12. S	

16
Reconstruction

KEY TOPICS

- ✓ **Advocating the "Lost Cause"**
- ✓ **Reconstruction's Impact**
- ✓ **Reconstruction's Phases**
- ✓ **Reconstruction's Legacy**

CHAPTER OUTLINE

I. White Southerners and the Ghosts of the Confederacy, 1865

II. More than Freedom: African American Aspirations in 1865
    A. Education
    B. "Forty Acres and a Mule"
    C. Migration to Cities
    D. Faith and Freedom

III. Federal Reconstruction, 1865–1870
    A. Presidential Reconstruction, 1865–1867
    B. Congressional Reconstruction, 1867–1870
    C. Southern Republican Governments, 1867–1870

IV. Counter-Reconstruction, 1870–1874
    A. The Uses of Violence
    B. Northern Indifference
    C. Liberal Republicans and the Election of 1872
    D. Economic Transformation

V. Redemption, 1874–1877
    A. The Democrats' Violent Resurgence
    B. The Weak Federal Response
    C. The Election of 1876 and the Compromise of 1877
    D. The Memory of Reconstruction

VI. The Failed Promise of Reconstruction
    A. Modest Gains and Future Victories

VII. Conclusion

SELF-TESTING

Multiple Choice: In the blanks below, write the letter of the BEST response.

1. _____ Among the problems faced by the South at the end of the Civil War was (were)
   a. long unattended cropland.
   b. destroyed infrastructure.
   c. a worthless currency.
   d. all of these problems.

2. _____ For most southern whites, their psychological response to defeat was to
   a. deny that military defeat had actually occurred.
   b. place blame for their defeat on their military leaders, especially Robert E. Lee.
   c. acknowledge that slavery had, in fact, been morally indefensible and that their defeat was deserved.
   d. elevate their rebellion to a noble and holy crusade.
   e. allow (though grudgingly) freed slaves to assume social equality.

3. _____ Following the Civil War, black southerners
   a. framed the war in biblical terms.
   b. wanted land, civil rights, and education—but also to be left alone.
   c. moved to the West and to northern cities.
   d. became tenant sharecroppers, usually on the land of their old masters.
   e. did all of these things.

4. _____ Following the Civil War, northern whites
   a. put the war into history books and moved on.
   b. became preoccupied with their business and industry.
   c. became less and less interested in the plight of the post-war South.
   d. could not figure out who should control the reconstruction process.
   e. did all of these things.

5. _____ Because of segregation, the "training ground" for generations of African American political, economic, and social leadership was often the
   a. years of Radical Republican rule.
   b. Freedmen's Bureau.
   c. public school system.
   d. black churches.
   e. local factory.

6. _____ Lincoln's lenient policy regarding reconstruction was called the
   a. Ten Percent Plan.
   b. Freedmen's Bureau.
   c. Wade Davis Plan.
   d. Southern Homestead Act.
   e. Half-way Covenant.

7. ____ Which post-war amendment gave black males the right to vote?
   a. Thirteenth
   b. Fourteenth
   c. Fifteenth
   d. All of these amendments were involved in granting black males the right to vote.

8. ____ When Congress took over the Reconstruction process, they
   a. created military districts in the South.
   b. disenfranchised many white southerners who had supported the Confederacy.
   c. made it more difficult for states to be re-admitted to the Union.
   d. secured freedmen's right to vote.
   e. accomplished all of these.

9. ____ Andrew Johnson was
   a. impeached by the House of Representatives but acquitted by the Senate.
   b. neither impeached by the House of Representatives nor acquitted by the Senate.
   c. impeached by the House of Representatives, convicted by the Senate, and removed from office.
   d. re-elected in 1868 for a full term of his own.

10. ____ The term "bloody shirt" referred to a
   a. cherished heirloom owned by the widow of Abraham Lincoln.
   b. Civil War-era relic on display at the Smithsonian Institute.
   c. campaign technique employed by post-war Republicans to remind voters of the Democrats' "treason" during the Civil War era.
   d. secret identifying signal employed by members of the Ku Klux Klan.

11. ____ Native white southerners who defied neighbors and joined the Republican ranks were called
   a. carpetbaggers.
   b. renegades.
   c. redeemers.
   d. things that cannot be repeated.
   e. scalawags.

12. ____ Most of the "carpetbaggers" who arrived in the South wanted to line their pockets at southerners' expense.
   a. True
   b. False

13. ____ There were no African American members of Congress until the 1930s.
   a. True
   b. False

14. ____ Republicans in the South fell into disharmony and out of power because of
   a. the liberal use of political patronage.
   b. high state-tax rates to fund their activist agendas.
   c. class and racial tensions.
   d. all of these situations.

15. _____ The initial (though short-lived) purpose of the Ku Klux Klan was to be a
    a. forum for political discussion.
    b. social club.
    c. Democratic "think tank."
    d. terrorist group advocating white supremacy.

16. _____ By 1870, "liberal" Republicans were advocating all of the following EXCEPT
    a. civil service reform.
    b. higher tariff rates to promote southern industry.
    c. an end to federal land grants for railroads.
    d. a general amnesty for white people.

17. _____ The presidential election of 1876 was decided by
    a. the popular vote.
    b. the electoral vote.
    c. the House of Representatives.
    d. a coin toss.
    e. a specially created commission.

18. _____ For generations, white southerners employed the "memory of reconstruction" to
    a. mean "redemption" from black rule and federal oppression.
    b. underscore the period, as they did the war itself, as a glorious crusade.
    c. turn textbooks and movies into propaganda.
    d. nurture racism in generations of southerners.
    e. accomplish all of these.

Chronological Arrangement: Re-arrange the list of events below by re-writing each item in correct chronological sequence into the blanks provided.

Ku Klux Klan founded   _____

Compromise of 1877   _____

Panic of 1873   _____

Ulysses Grant elected president   _____

Tenure of Office Act passed   _____

Lincoln proposes the Ten Percent Plan   _____

House impeaches Andrew Johnson   _____

Election of 1876 outcome contested   _____

Fifteenth Amendment ratified   _____

Andrew Johnson becomes president   _____

Essay: Read each of the following questions, take some time to organize your thoughts, then compose thorough, meaningful answers for each.

1. List and discuss the major problems faced by the United States at the end of the Civil War.

2. In what ways did post-war African Americans adjust to their new freedom?

3. How did Andrew Johnson's background and life experiences contribute to his version of Reconstruction?

4. Describe the struggle that developed between President Johnson and Congress over Reconstruction. How was the problem "resolved"?

5. How did blacks achieve—and then lose—political power in the South following the war?

6. Discuss the rise of white supremacist groups such as the Ku Klux Klan.

7. Why did the North eventually turn its back on the South?

8. How did the presidential election of 1876 relate to the end of Reconstruction?

9. Why could it be said that the South "won" the Civil War?

10. In your opinion, what could have been done differently to make Reconstruction a success?

Matching: Match each description in the left column with the Reconstruction-era political party most likely to reflect it.

1. _____ Most southern white voters

2. _____ Most southern black voters

3. _____ Carpetbaggers

4. _____ Klan members

5. _____ Used religious metaphors to explain their position

6. _____ Manipulated memories of Reconstruction to maintain power

7. _____ Scalawags

8. _____ Created southern solidarity by race-baiting and violence

9. _____ Benefited from the post-war economic boom

10. _____ Southern black legislators

11. _____ Waved the "bloody shirt"

12. _____ Claimed presidential victory in 1876

A. Democratic

B. Republican

C. Both Parties

Matching: Match each description in the left column with the person it most likely describes. (Beware: Not all names will be used!)

1. _____ Though he freed his nation's serfs, he did not free them from a plight similar to African Americans'.

2. _____ His "Field Order No. 15" fueled rumors that blacks would be receiving "forty acres and a mule."

3. _____ Returned confiscated land to Confederates; vetoed reconstruction measures; opposed Fourteenth Amendment.

4. _____ Lincoln's—then Johnson's—Secretary of War; his firing led to Johnson's impeachment.

5. _____ Suffragist who opposed the Fifteenth Amendment because it extended the vote only to males.

6. _____ Was declared the winner in 1876—in exchange for the end of Reconstruction in the South.

7. _____ Turned Democratic Tammany Hall into a machine that robbed New York of $100 million.

8. _____ Northern general; though elected president twice, his two terms were tarnished by scandals.

9. _____ Won the popular vote in 1876, yet did not get to deliver the inaugural speech.

A. Alexander II

B. Susan B. Anthony

C. George A. Custer

D. William ("Boss") Tweed

E. Robert E. Lee

F. Nathan B. Forrest

G. Ulysses Grant

H. Rutherford B. Hayes

I. Ivan the Terrible

J. Andrew Johnson

K. Kirby Smith

L. James Longstreet

M. Edwin M. Stanton

N. Nicholas II

O. Oliver Howard

P. Peter the Great

Q. Victoria

R. Edmond Ruffin

S. Samuel J. Tilden

T. William T. Sherman

MULTIPLE CHOICE ANSWERS:

1. E	11. E
2. D	12. B
3. E	13. B
4. E	14. D
5. D	15. B
6. A	16. B
7. C	17. E
8. E	18. E
9. A	
10. C	

CHRONOLOGICAL ARRANGEMENT ANSWERS:

Lincoln proposes the Ten Percent Plan

Andrew Johnson becomes president

Ku Klux Klan founded

Tenure of Office Act passed

House impeaches Andrew Johnson

Ulysses Grant first elected president

Fifteenth Amendment ratified

Panic of 1873

Election of 1876 outcome contested

Compromise of 1877

MATCHING ANSWERS:

1. A		7. B	
2. B		8. A	
3. B		9. B	
4. A		10. B	
5. A		11. B	
6. A		12. C	

MATCHING ANSWERS:

1. A
2. T
3. J
4. M
5. B
6. H
7. D
8. G
9. S